PENGUIN CLASSICS

A LITTLE LARGER THAN THE ENTIRE
UNIVERSE: SELECTED POEMS

FERNANDO PESSOA was born in Lisbon in 1888 and spent most of his childhood in Durban, South Africa. In 1905 he returned to Lisbon to enroll in college but eventually dropped out, preferring to study on his own. He made a modest living translating the foreign correspondence of various commercial firms, and wrote obsessively—in English, Portuguese, and French. He self-published several chapbooks of his English poems in 1918 and 1921, and regularly contributed his Portuguese poems to literary reviews. *Mensagem*, a collection of poems on patriotic themes, won a prize in a national competition in 1934. Pessoa wrote much of his greatest poetry in the guise of his three main "heteronyms"—Alberto Caeiro, Álvaro de Campos, and Ricardo Reis—whose fully fleshed biographies he invented, giving them different writing styles and points of view. He created dozens of other writerly personas, including the assistant bookkeeper Bernardo Soares, fictional author of *The Book of Disquiet*. Although Pessoa was acknowledged as an intellectual and a poet, his literary genius went largely unrecognized until after his death in 1935.

RICHARD ZENITH lives in Lisbon, where he works as a freelance writer, translator, and critic. His translations include Galician–Portuguese troubadour songs, poems by Carlos Drummond de Andrade, Pessoa's *The Book of Disquiet*, and *Fernando Pessoa and Co.—Selected Poems*, which won the 1999 American PEN Award for Poetry in Translation. He is the author of *Pessoa: A Biography*, a Pulitzer Prize finalist.

T0003283

FERNANDO PESSOA

A Little Larger Than the Entire Universe

SELECTED POEMS

Edited and Translated by
RICHARD ZENITH

PENGUIN BOOKS

PENGUIN BOOKS

An imprint of Penguin Random House LLC
penguinrandomhouse.com

First published in Penguin Books 2006
This edition with revisions throughout published 2023

Translation, introduction, and notes copyright © 2006 by Richard Zenith
Penguin Random House supports copyright. Copyright fuels creativity, encourages diverse voices,
promotes free speech, and creates a vibrant culture. Thank you for buying an authorized edition of
this book and for complying with copyright laws by not reproducing, scanning, or distributing any
part of it in any form without permission. You are supporting writers and allowing Penguin Random
House to continue to publish books for every reader.

Grateful acknowledgment is made for permission to reprint "My gaze is clear like a sunflower,"
"I'm a keeper of sheep," "I got off the train," and "Autopsychography" from *Fernando Pessoa & Co.,*
edited and translated by Richard Zenith. Copyright © 1998 by Richard Zenith.
Used by permission of Grove/Atlantic, Inc.

LIBRARY OF CONGRESS CATALOGING-IN-PUBLICATION DATA
Pessoa, Fernando, 1888–1935.
A little larger than the entire universe : selected poems / Fernando Pessoa ;
edited and translated by Richard Zenith.
p. cm.
Includes bibliographical references.
ISBN 9780143039556 (paperback)
I. Zenith, Richard. II. Title.
PQ9261.P417A6 2006
861'.141—dc22   2005056561

Printed in the United States of America
28th Printing
Set in Sabon

Contents

RICARDO REIS   81

Introduction

Old and enormous are the stars.
Old and small is the heart, and it
Holds more than all the stars, being,
Without space, greater than the vast expanse.
FROM PESSOA'S RUBA'IYAT
IN THE MANNER OF OMAR KHAYYAM

Much has been made of Fernando Pessoa's last name, which means, in Portuguese, "person." Famous for splitting himself into a multitude of literary alter egos he dubbed "heteronyms"—more than mere pseudonyms, since he endowed them with biographies, religious and political views, and diverse writing styles—Pessoa claimed that he, within that self-generated universe, was the least real person of all. "I've divided all my humanness among the various authors whom I've served as literary executor," explained Pessoa in a passage about the genesis and evolution of his fictional writer friends. "I subsist," he explains further on in the same passage, "as a kind of medium of myself, but I'm less real than the others, less substantial, less personal, and easily influenced by them all." The lack of any certainty about who he is, or even if he is, stands out as a major theme in Pessoa's poetry, and he uses the heteronyms to accentuate his ironic self-detachment. In a prose piece signed by Álvaro de Campos, a dandyish naval engineer and the most provocative of the heteronyms, we read that "Fernando Pessoa, strictly speaking, doesn't exist."

Pessoa's last name, in light of his existential self-doubts, is especially appreciated by the French, since *personne* means not only "person" but also, as in the phrase *Je suis personne*, "nobody." Pessoa, however, was very definitely, or very indefinitely, *somebody*. And that his last name meant "person" was surely not incidental to his monomaniacal concern with his own personhood, its multiplication and its perpetuation, through his literary oeuvre. I mean that Pessoa, who may or may not have believed in God but who very much believed in destiny and in destiny's symbols and signposts, had his name to live up to. It was, in a slight way, determining.

More determining, of course, was the cultural and family setting in which Pessoa, as a person and an artist, developed. For all his obsession with the inner life, he was keenly aware of how outer circumstances shape and define who we inwardly are. In a prose piece titled "Environment," signed by Campos and published in 1927, he observed: "A place is what it is because of its location. Where we are is who we are." But while he recognized the defining role of environment, Pessoa was by no means a hard-core determinist. In a longer version of the piece just cited, he wrote: "The man who jumped over the wall had a wall to jump over." The wall, being a necessary condition, was in that sense determining, but not compelling, since the man could choose whether or not to jump it.

Pessoa's particular genius is at least partly explained by the two environments that shaped him—Lisbon, where he spent his first seven years and the whole of his adult life, and Durban, South Africa, where he lived during his intellectually and emotionally formative years, from age seven to seventeen. Pessoa's basic personality was no doubt set in place before he moved with his mother from Lisbon to Durban, but his literary output was clearly the product of the meeting, or clash, of those two environments and their different languages, their different cultures. It's as if English culture—and white Durban, at the time, was more thoroughly, traditionally English than England itself—were a wall that the young, displaced Pessoa successfully jumped over, while remaining forever and utterly Portuguese. Although Pessoa attended all-white schools, people of European descent (British, mostly) made up less than half of Durban's population, with Indians accounting for about 30 percent and indigenous Zulus close to 25 percent of the town's inhabitants. The boy's contact with nonwhites was limited but made for a precocious awareness of humanity's diversity.

Fernando António Nogueira Pessoa was born in 1888 on June
13, the feast day of St. Anthony and an official holiday in Lis-
bon, where elaborate festivities are organized in honor of the
saint and in honor of the city itself. St. Anthony's day is Lis-
bon's day, and no birthday could be more appropriate for Pes-
soa, who is his native city's quintessential writer. Even more, I
would argue, than Kafka is Prague's writer, or Joyce is Dublin's
writer. Though Kafka spent his whole life in Prague, the city
isn't much felt in his writing, except in the diaries. Joyce, on the
other hand, wrote obsessively about the city of his birth, but
from memory, having spent very little time there as an adult.
Pessoa rarely left Lisbon as an adult, and he wrote about the
city both directly (especially in *The Book of Disquiet*) and out
of imaginative memory, through the voice of footloose Álvaro
de Campos, who on return visits from Britain (where he was
supposedly living) produced the nostalgia-imbued "Lisbon Re-
visited (1923)" and "Lisbon Revisited (1926)," two of his most
striking poems.

Both of Pessoa's parents fostered his cultural development.
The family lived just opposite Lisbon's opera house, where as
a small boy Pessoa may have attended a performance or two
with his father, an impassioned music critic as well as a gov-
ernment employee. Pessoa's mother, who was from the Azores,
was unusually well educated and taught her son to read and
write at a very young age. But Pessoa's early Lisbon years were
also, ultimately, marked by loss and separation. One month
after his fifth birthday, his father died from tuberculosis, and
six months later his baby brother died. Between the two deaths,
the family moved to smaller quarters. In the following year Pes-
soa's mother met her second husband, a naval officer who left
Lisbon in February 1895 to take up a new post in Mozambique.
Eight months later he was appointed the Portuguese consul in
Durban, the largest town of the English colony of Natal.

The prospect of his mother moving to Africa to be with her
future husband and of Pessoa perhaps being left behind with
relatives prompted his first poem, in July of 1895:

To My Dear Mother

Here I am in Portugal,
In the lands where I was born.
However much I love them,
I love you even more.

This quatrain is often cited as a demonstration of Pessoa's filial
devotion, but it is also proof of his unusual affection for his
homeland—"unusual," since a seven-year-old whose personal
relationships are mostly with his immediate family could hardly
be expected to have a very clear idea of what a nation is, much
less feel emotionally attached to one. Throughout his life Pes-
soa, though he would criticize the Portuguese for being provin-
cial and revile Portugal's political leaders and its economic
system, was fiercely loyal to the country of his birth.

In February of 1896 Pessoa and his mother, married to her
second husband by proxy two months earlier, arrived at Dur-
ban, where the boy was enrolled in a primary school run by
French nuns. Three years later he entered Durban High School,
where he received a demanding, first-rate English education.
Pessoa, despite being a foreigner, immediately stood out as
a brilliant student, and when he sat for the Matriculation
Examination of the University of the Cape of Good Hope, in
1903, he won the Queen Victoria Prize for the best essay in En-
glish. There were 899 examinees.

Pessoa's African experience was basically a bookish experi-
ence. Though liked well enough by his classmates, he did not
participate much in sports or cultivate many friends, and neither
the town of Durban nor the surrounding country seems to have
left much of an impression on him. Among the hundreds of
literary pieces he wrote during his adult life, Africa was almost
never explicitly referred to until the year of his death, when in
"Un Soir à Lima," a poem evoking his mother playing the piano
at home in Durban, he recalls listening to her from next to the
window while he gazed outside at the vast African landscape,
lit up by the moon. Pessoa's environment, while in Africa, was
mostly that of English literature: Shakespeare and Milton, the

romantic poets—Shelley, Byron, Keats, Wordsworth—and Dickens and Carlyle for prose. He also read and admired Poe.

Pessoa very nearly became an English writer. What "saved" him for Portuguese literature was a year-long trip that the family—Pessoa, his mother and stepfather, and several children born to the new couple—made to Portugal in 1901–02. It was there that Pessoa wrote his earliest known poems in Portuguese (besides the above-mentioned quatrain to his mother), one of which was published in a Lisbon newspaper in 1902. Both in Lisbon and on the island of Terceira, where the family went to visit Pessoa's mother's sister, the budding adolescent, who suddenly had a lot of time with no schoolwork to fill it, invented a series of elaborate, make-believe newspapers containing news, jokes, commentary, and poems credited to a team of fictional journalists, several of whom he invented biographies for.

Back in Durban, Pessoa, at age fifteen, invented Charles Robert Anon, his first alter ego to sign a substantial body of creative writing, including poems, short stories, and essays. C. R. Anon had several "friends," including Karl P. Effield and Horace Faber, who also signed poems and prose pieces written by Pessoa in English. But the most prolific English-language heteronym, Alexander Search, would not emerge until 1906, one year after Pessoa's definitive return to Lisbon. Supposedly born in Lisbon on the same day as Pessoa, Search would express, like Anon before him, the intellectual concerns and existential anxieties of a young man on the threshold of becoming an adult. Pessoa, in a certain way, remained forever on that threshold. Instead of getting down to the practical business of living, he continued to wrestle with theoretical problems and the big questions: the existence of God, the meaning of life and the meaning of death, good vs. evil, reality vs. appearance, the idea (is it just an idea?) of love, the limits of consciousness, and so on. All of which was rich fodder for his poetry, thriving as it did on ideas more than on actual experience.

In December of 1904 Pessoa took the Intermediate Arts Examination and received the highest score in Natal, which would have earned him a government grant to study at Oxford or Cambridge, but there was a hitch: applicants had to have spent the four previous years at a Natal school. Because of the trip he made to Lisbon in 1901–02, Pessoa was disqualified. Instead of going to England, the precocious seventeen-year-old returned to Lisbon, where he studied literature at a college for almost two years before dropping out. He earned no academic credits, having missed the first year's exams due to illness, and the second year's exams due to a student strike. While at the college and afterwards, he spent long hours at the National Library studying Greek and German philosophy, world religions, psychology, and evolutionary thought (cultural and social more than biological). He read a wide range of Western literature, especially in French (Hugo, Baudelaire, Flaubert, and Rollinat, among others), in English, and in Portuguese, his readings in this last language filling a serious lacuna in his South African education.

And he wrote steadily: poetry, fiction, philosophy, sociology, and literary criticism. During his first years back on home turf he very occasionally wrote in Portuguese, somewhat more often in French (Pessoa's solitary French heteronym, Jean Seul, emerged in 1908), and most of all in English. Pessoa's ambition, even after he had returned to Lisbon, was to become a great poet in English, and he continued to produce poems in that language up until one week before his death. In 1917 he submitted a book-length collection of verse, *The Mad Fiddler*, to a London publisher who quickly rejected it, but one of the book's poems appeared three years later in the prestigious magazine *Athenaeum*. In 1918 Pessoa self-published two chapbooks of his English poems, with two more following in 1921, and these received guarded praise from the British press. About his *35 Sonnets* (1918), a note in the *Times Literary Supplement* remarked: "Mr. Pessoa's command of English is less remarkable than his knowledge of Elizabethan English. . . . The sonnets . . . will interest many by reason of their ultra-Shakespearean Shakespeareanisms, and their Tudor tricks of repetition, involution and antithesis, no less than by the worth of what they have to say." The *Glasgow Herald* was also complimentary, but noted "a certain crabbedness of speech, due to an imitation of a Shakespearean trick."

Pessoa's English was the English of the books he read, and

these included contemporary novelists, such as H. G. Wells, Sir Arthur Conan Doyle, and W. W. Jacobs, but it lacked the brutal naturalness of a mother tongue. His English, though fluent in the literal sense of that word, was *his* English—a more literary, slightly archaic, and occasionally stilted variety of the language. The poetry he wrote in it is interesting for the ideas and emotions it contains, as well as for its skillful use of poetic devices, but like a piano out of tune or a camera out of focus, Pessoa's English introduces a slight distortion that mars the overall effect.

The English language provided a modest but dependable income for Pessoa, who made his living by translating and by drafting letters in English (and occasionally in French) for Portuguese firms doing business abroad. He also tried to do business himself, mainly as an agent for Portuguese mining companies in search of investment capital from Britain and elsewhere, but it doesn't seem that he ever cut any profitable deals.

Where English best served Pessoa, however, was in the poetry and prose he wrote in Portuguese. If Anglo-American literature influenced *what* Pessoa wrote, the English language itself influenced *how* he wrote. English is more apt than the Romance languages to repeat words—for the sake of clarity, for syntactical straightforwardness, or for a rhetorical effect—and Pessoa followed this usage in Portuguese (in *The Book of Disquiet*, for instance). And whereas Pessoa's English sonnets employ a convoluted syntax derived from his Elizabethan models, modern English seems to have inspired the directness of expression that characterizes the poetry attributed to Alberto Caeiro and Álvaro de Campos.

After Pessoa's first wave of poetic creation in Portuguese, with about fifteen surviving poems dating from when he was thirteen and fourteen, he didn't go back to writing poetry in his native tongue (except for an odd example here and there) until he was twenty, three years after returning to Lisbon. By 1911 he was writing as much poetry in Portuguese as in English, and a year later he published, in a Porto-based magazine, two large articles on the state of recent Portuguese poetry from, respectively, a "sociological" and a "psychological" point of view. Fernando Pessoa was coming into his own. In 1913 he published his first piece of creative prose, a passage from *The Book of Disquiet*, which he would work on for the rest of his life, and in 1914 he published, in Portuguese, his first poems as an adult. That was the year when four of Portugal's greatest twentieth-century poets were born: Alberto Caeiro, Álvaro de Campos, Ricardo Reis, and Fernando Pessoa himself.

Alberto Caeiro, who emerged from Pessoa's soul in the late winter of 1914, lived in the country, had no formal education, and said he wanted to see things as they are, without any philosophy:

> *What matters is to know how to see,*
> *To know how to see without thinking,*
> *To know how to see when seeing*
> *And not think when seeing*
> *Nor see when thinking.*

Caeiro claimed to be "the only poet of Nature," but his vision of nature was ideal, his appreciation of it abstract, and his poetry is almost pure philosophy. To *talk about seeing* things directly is tantamount to *no longer seeing* them directly. Caeiro was a moment of poetic nirvana, an impossibility embodied in weightless verses of rare, crystalline beauty. Pessoa called him the Master and reported—twenty years later—that Alberto Caeiro "appeared" in him on March 8, 1914, the "triumphal day" of his life, when he wrote all at once, "in a kind of ecstasy," over thirty of the forty-nine poems that make up *The Keeper of Sheep*, Caeiro's (and Pessoa's) most sublime poetic work. From the manuscripts we know that this account is not quite true, but close to thirty poems were written over the course of two weeks in March of that year, and later poems written in Caeiro's name rarely attain the astonishing clarity of that initial outpouring.

"Born" on April 16, 1889, Caeiro was in various ways a tribute to Pessoa's best friend, the writer Mário de Sá-Carneiro (1890–1916). *Caeiro* is *Carneiro* (the Portuguese word for "sheep") without the *carne*, or "flesh," and Alberto Caeiro, by profession, was an idealized shepherd ("I've never kept sheep / But it's as if I kept them," he explains at the beginning of *The Keeper of Sheep*). His zodiac sign, naturally enough, was Aries, the ram. Sá-Carneiro committed suicide in 1916, a few weeks before his twenty-sixth birthday, and Alberto Caeiro, according to his "biography," also died young, at age twenty-five or twenty-six, from tuberculosis. About one as about the other Pessoa wrote: "Those whom the gods love die young."

Caeiro was initially conceived not just as "Nature's poet" but as a multifaceted modernist, responsible for "intersectionist" poems inspired by cubism and for a planned series of "futurist odes." But the intersectionist poems were ultimately assigned to Pessoa–himself, and the futurist ambitions were transferred to Álvaro de Campos, who came into being in early June of 1914, an offshoot of Alberto Caeiro. The organic relationship between the two is reflected in their similar-sounding names. Not only that, *de campos* means "from the fields": Álvaro came from the fields where Alberto tended his imaginary or metaphorical sheep.

Campos, according to his script, was born in the Algarve in 1890, studied naval engineering in Glasgow, traveled to the Far East, lived for a few years in England, where he courted both young men and women, and finally returned to Portugal, settling down in Lisbon. Campos's early poems, such as the "Triumphal Ode," celebrated machines and the modern age with loud and sustained exuberance. His later poems are shorter and melancholy in tone, but the basic Campos creed remains:

> To feel everything in every way,
> To live everything from all sides,
> To be the same thing in all ways possible at the same time,
> To realize in oneself all humanity at all moments
> In one scattered, extravagant, complete and aloof moment.

Álvaro de Campos was the most public heteronym, airing his views on political and literary matters in articles and interviews published (apparently with the help of Pessoa) in Lisbon-based magazines. He was fond of contradicting the opinions of his creator, whom he censured for being too rational-minded, with the "mania of believing that things can be proved," and he also enjoyed meddling in Pessoa's social life. He would occasionally turn up in lieu of Fernando at appointments, to the chagrin and ire of those who were not amused by such antics.

Ricardo Reis, the third in the trio of Pessoa's full-fledged heteronyms, also emerged in June of 1914, probably a few days after Álvaro de Campos. A physician and classicist, whom Pessoa defined as a "Greek Horace writing in Portuguese," Reis composed metered, nonrhyming odes about the vanity of life and the need to accept our fate:

> Since we do nothing in this confused world
> That lasts or that, lasting, is worth anything,
> And even what's useful for us we lose
>   All too soon, with our own lives,
> Let us prefer the pleasure of the moment
> To an absurd concern with the future . . .

Ricardo Reis, according to his creator, was born in 1887 in Porto, which became the focal point of the surviving monarchist forces after the founding of the Portuguese Republic, in 1910. In 1919 the monarchists took control of Porto but were soon defeated, at which point Reis, a royalist sympathizer (his last name means "kings"), fled to Brazil, where he presumably lived out the rest of his days, though there is, among the thousands of papers left by Pessoa at his death, an address for Dr. Reis in Peru.

All three heteronyms were expressions of "sensationism," one of the literary movements (like intersectionism, mentioned above) invented by Pessoa and taken up by his modernist writer friends. In a passage signed by Thomas Crosse—a fictional English critic and translator created a year or two after Caeiro, Reis, and Campos—Pessoa neatly differentiated among the three poets and the types of sensationism they represented: "Caeiro has one discipline: things must be felt as they are. Ricardo Reis has another kind of discipline: things must be felt, not only as they are, but also so as to fall in with a certain ideal of classic measure and rule. In Álvaro de Campos things must simply be felt."

The year 1914 also marked a turning point in the work of the poet who signed himself Fernando Pessoa but who was not the same person as the flesh-and-blood Pessoa known to be living at this time with his aunt Anica. Álvaro de Campos reports that Pessoa–himself, after meeting Caeiro in 1914 and hearing him recite *The Keeper of Sheep*, experienced a "spiritual shock" that resulted in his most original work to date.

Beyond all the self-fictionalization, there occurred in fact a profound transformation, and culmination, in Pessoa's literary art. Caeiro, Campos, and Reis were the most visible result of that transformation, for they represented something totally new, but heteronymy as such was no novelty. Besides the aforementioned heteronyms who wrote in English and French, one of the Portuguese journalists invented in Pessoa's adolescence—Dr. Pancrácio—signed six poems, two epigrams, and various riddles, while Dr. Gaudêncio Nabos, a fictional author of humorous prose pieces and poems who originated in Durban, remained active until at least 1913. Vicente Guedes, one of the first heteronyms to write extensively in Portuguese, emerged already in 1909. Heteronymy, in fact, goes all the way back to Pessoa's infancy, when as a six-year-old he wrote letters to himself signed by a personage called the Chevalier de Pas.

Pessoa described his artistic enterprise as "a drama divided into people instead of into acts." He created, in other words, a series of characters but no play for them to act in. What they played out, in a certain way, was the life that their shy, retiring creator chose not to live in the physical world. "I've created in myself various personalities," he explained in a passage from *The Book of Disquiet*. "Each of my dreams, as soon as I start dreaming it, is immediately incarnated in another person, who is then the one dreaming it, and not I. To create, I've destroyed myself. . . . I'm the naked stage where various actors act out various plays."

It is no wonder that Pessoa, who considered himself to be "essentially a dramatist," admired Shakespeare and Milton

(whose *Paradise Lost* is practically a verse drama) above all
other writers. Pessoa published one short, ethereal play, O *Mar-
inheiro* (The Mariner), which he termed a "static drama," and
he left a score of unfinished plays, in Portuguese and English,
but only the "static" ones, where no action is expected, are of
much interest. Like Robert Browning, a poet he much read and
appreciated, Pessoa put his dramatic instincts to better use in
his poetry. But he went further than the English poet, for his
dramatis personae were more than poetic subjects; he made
them into quasi-autonomous poets.

All of this becomes fascinating when we delve deeper into the
heteronymous system, which includes an astrologer, a friar, a
philosopher, various translators, diarists, a nobleman who com-
mits suicide, and a hunchback girl dying of tuberculosis. Yet I
still haven't explained (if it's possible to explain) what caused
the explosion in 1914 that transformed Pessoa into a great
writer. I have mentioned the vast range of literature and learn-
ing that the writer-in-progress absorbed as a schoolboy and as a
young man, during and after his abbreviated university career,
and to these ingredients one must add the French decadents and
symbolists (Baudelaire, Mallarmé, Verlaine, and Rimbaud),
whom he read around 1906 and 1907. Next he steeped him-
self in Portuguese poetry, from its earliest manifestations in
thirteenth-century troubadour songs (some of which he trans-
lated into English) to contemporary work by Teixeira de Pasco-
aes (1877–1952) and other *saudosista* poets, who promoted a
nationalistic nostalgia as a spiritual value and a creative energy.
But what finally seems to have ignited this complex mixture of
linguistic and literary acquisitions, provoking a kind of alchem-
ical reaction, was Walt Whitman, arguably the single greatest
influence on Pessoa's poetry and, more generally, on Pessoa the
artist.

It is not, as several critics have supposed, that Pessoa was a
"son" of the American poet. The Whitmanian influence is clearly
discernible in the poetry of Alberto Caeiro and Álvaro de Cam-
pos, but neither heteronym is a mere derivative, for they could
not have existed without numerous other inputs from Pessoa's
rich literary background. Whitman, though, seems to have acted

as a key to open up Pessoa and the power of his own personality. *Song of Myself* is a song of the whole cosmos—the cosmos felt and substantiated in the self—and it was this audacity, this chutzpah, that galvanized Pessoa and his heteronymous cosmos, which otherwise might not have been more than a curious psychological phenomenon and stylistic exercise, without real literary consequence. Pessoa indicated as much in a two-part article, "Notes for a Non-Aristotelian Aesthetics," signed by heteronym Álvaro de Campos and published in 1925. In it the naval engineer advocates an aesthetics based on inner, personal force—the force of personality—rather than on outward beauty and, concomitantly, an art based on sensibility rather than on intelligence. The article ends with the bold affirmation that "up until now . . . there have been only three genuine manifestations of non-Aristotelian art. The first is in the astonishing poems of Walt Whitman; the second is in the even more astonishing poems of my master Caeiro; the third is in the two odes—the 'Triumphal Ode' and the 'Maritime Ode'—that I published in *Orpheu*."

Orpheu was a literary review founded in 1915 by Pessoa, his friend Mário de Sá-Carneiro, and other vanguard writers and artists. In its brief life—only two issues were published—it introduced modernism into Portugal. Several members of the group were in contact with the cubists and futurists in Paris, while Pessoa, through his readings, kept abreast of the latest literary currents in Britain, Spain, France, and elsewhere (he obtained copies, for instance, of *Blast*, a vorticist review where Ezra Pound published poems in 1914). *Orpheu* prompted reactions of outrage and ridicule in the press and the literary establishment, but the genius of Pessoa's work was quietly recognized.

In 1917 Pessoa published, in the name of Álvaro de Campos, an inflammatory *Ultimatum* in the one and only issue of *Portugal Futurista*, which was immediately seized from the newsstands by the police. Portugal supported the Allies in the war, and while Pessoa-Campos's ranting manifesto was not pro-German, it heaped as much abuse on the British, French, and other Allied leaders as on Wilhelm II and Bismarck. After lambasting the present age for its "incapacity to create anything great," Campos's manifesto calls for the "abolition of the dogma of personality" and affirms that "no artist should have just one personality," since "the greatest artist will be the one who least defines himself and who writes in the most genres with the most contradictions and discrepancies." The greatest artist, in other words, will have multiple personalities ("fifteen or twenty," states the manifesto farther on), like Fernando Pessoa.

This was not the first time that Pessoa predicted his own artistic greatness. In the articles on Portuguese poetry that he published in 1912 he envisioned the imminent emergence of a "Great Poet" who would overshadow even Luís de Camões, universally regarded as Portugal's premier poet. It is clear, in retrospect, that Pessoa was setting the stage for his own grand entrance (or entrances, thanks to the heteronyms). But personal greatness, in the form of literary immortality, was only part of his dream. In those same articles from 1912, Pessoa also foresaw the dawning, in Portugal, of a "New Renaissance," which would spread from the nation's borders to the rest of Europe, as had the Italian Renaissance centuries earlier.

Pessoa would subsequently recast his vision of a Portuguese Renaissance in the doctrine of the Fifth Empire, a new take on an old prophecy, from the Book of Daniel, chapter 2. The prophet's interpretation of a dream of Nebuchadnezzar, King of Babylon, had traditionally been understood as a history of the Western world's great military empires—Babylonian, Persian, Greek, and Roman, with the fifth sometimes being understood as the British Empire. Pessoa, adopting a "spiritual" or cultural point of view, understood the five empires to be those of Greece, Rome, the Christian West, post-Renaissance Europe, and—on the near horizon—Portugal. The idea was that Portugal, through its language and culture, and most especially through its literature, would dominate the rest of Europe. An "imperialism of poets," specifies one of the passages Pessoa wrote on the subject.

Pessoa's nationalism was as constructive as it was ardent. He had no illusions about Portugal's relative backwardness vis-à-vis the rest of Europe, and his goal was to make it catch up. He took the British and French cultures as models to emulate, at least in certain respects, and the English-speaking world as the best outlet for promoting Portuguese culture abroad. Already in 1909 he had planned to publish, in a printing office founded with a small inheritance left by his paternal grandmother, a long list of classic and contemporary Portuguese works translated into English, as well as a collection of foreign classics, including Shakespeare's complete works, in Portuguese. The Empreza Ibis, as the press was called, was also supposed to publish magazines, political treatises, and scientific works, and—last but not least—numerous works by Pessoa and his heteronyms, in English and in Portuguese.

Pessoa's personal literary ambitions were, as he saw it, in perfect accord with his concern to make Portugal more cosmopolitan and to promote its culture abroad. His writings aimed, either directly or by example, to educate the Portuguese, to make them more European. For their sheer originality and quality (Pessoa was never modest), his writings would convince foreigners of the worth and cleverness of contemporary Portuguese literature. Pessoa, by promoting his own work, felt that he was promoting Portugal. This rationale was perhaps justified, in view of his considerable literary talents, but his entrepreneurial skills were wanting, and economic difficulties forced the Empreza Ibis to close its doors forthwith.

During and immediately after World War I, Pessoa drew up plans for an even more grandiose enterprise—tentatively called Cosmópolis—whose mission would be to foster cultural and commercial exchange between Britain and Portugal. A conglomerate with offices in Lisbon and London, it would provide information for businessmen and travelers, translation and interpretation services, legal advice, publicity and public relations expertise, research and editorial assistance, and a host of other services. The Lisbon branch would also include a subsidiary company for promoting Portuguese products and encouraging new industries, a school offering courses in business training and cultural enrichment, and a publishing house that would publish not only books by contemporary authors but also literary classics in cheap editions, magazines, business directories, and guidebooks.

What finally emerged from all these plans, in 1920, was a small commercial agency and publishing house called Olisipo, which did little more than publish half a dozen books, including two chapbooks of Pessoa's English poems, a re-edition of a poetry collection by the openly homosexual António Botto, and a booklet by the even more stridently homosexual Raul Leal, whose *Sodoma Divinizada* (Sodom Deified) did exactly what its title promised. Conservative Catholic students launched a campaign against the "literature of Sodom," the two books were banned, and Pessoa counterattacked, through self-published manifestos that mocked the students' pretended morality and fervently defended his authors. This episode reveals another facet of Pessoa's program to shake up and educate Portuguese society and, if possible, European civilization in general, since a book like Raul Leal's would have caused public indignation throughout most of the continent. Though Pessoa tended to be conservative in his politics, his defense of an individual's right to free expression—even in sexual matters—was far advanced for his time.

In 1924 Pessoa founded *Athena*, whose five issues demonstrated, in exemplary fashion, how his literary self-promotion dovetailed with his concern to elevate Portuguese culture. The magazine, beginning with its title and elegant graphic presentation, was an ideal illustration of the New Renaissance presaged by Pessoa twelve years earlier and a showcase for the Great Poet—Fernando Pessoa—who was supposed to spearhead Portugal's cultural rebirth. It was in this exquisite publication—which included art reproductions, essays signed by Pessoa and by Álvaro de Campos, and translations by Pessoa of inscriptions from *The Greek Anthology*, poems of Edgar Allan Poe, and an excerpt from Walter Pater's essay on da Vinci—that Ricardo Reis and Alberto Caeiro were first revealed to the public, with a large selection of poems by each.

The neo-Greek revival that these two heteronyms were meant to foreshadow—Reis with the atmosphere of antiquity and abundant references to the gods in his odes, Caeiro with the "absolute objectivity" of his clear, direct seeing—was undergirded by "neopaganism," a philosophical and religious system embedded in their poetry and expounded on in theoretical texts signed by Reis and António Mora, a heteronym conceived as a "philosophical follower" of Caeiro.

To wonder if Pessoa believed in the pagan gods whose return he heralded and advocated for Portugal is like wondering if he "believed" in the heteronyms who embodied (especially Caeiro) or espoused (Reis and Mora) the neopagan cause. They and it were part of the same package, or rather, of the same dispersion, since what Pessoa did *not* believe in was unity. "Nature is parts without a whole" was, according to Pessoa, Caeiro's greatest, truest line of verse (from the forty-seventh poem of *The Keeper of Sheep*), and in a Reis ode he proposed that "as each fountain / Has its own deity, might not each man / Have a god all his own?" The phenomenon of heteronymy reflects Pessoa's conviction that even at the level of the self there is no unity, and if he championed the resurgence of paganism with its myriad gods, it is because he rejected the vision of an ultimate, otherworldly unity propounded by Christianity and other monotheistic religions. Which isn't to say that he did not *desire* unity. In the heteronymy of his fragmented self Pessoa, paradoxically, endeavored to construct a small but complete universe of interrelated parts forming a coherent whole. And his literary creations were all attempts to achieve a moment of unity, an instance of perfection, in the midst of the general chaos of existence.

Perhaps because of his nagging awareness of that chaos, Pessoa, notwithstanding his compulsion to doubt everything, believed as much as he could believe in a spiritual dimension. His religious attitude seems to be well expressed in the opening lines of a poem by Álvaro de Campos, whose later work tended to speak directly from his maker's heart:

> *I don't know if the stars rule the world*
> *Or if tarot or playing cards*
> *Can reveal anything.*
> *I don't know if the rolling of dice*
> *Can lead to any conclusion.*
> *But I also don't know*

If anything is attained
By living the way most people do.

5 January 1935

Though he didn't know what, if anything, is behind or beyond what we are and see, Pessoa was clearly not interested in "living the way most people do." He spent his entire life searching for the Truth, when he wasn't inventing it, and this search led him into a whole panoply of esoteric disciplines and occult practices. As far as the stars were concerned, he was an avid astrologer, having cast hundreds of charts for friends, family members, historical and cultural figures, and for himself. More significantly, he read dozens of books and wrote hundreds of pages on mysticism, on Hermetic traditions such as the Kabbalah, Rosicrucianism, and Freemasonry, and on Theosophy, alchemy, numerology, magic, and spiritism.

This interest in the occult combined with Pessoa's patriotic bent to produce what he called "mystical nationalism," expressed in his Fifth Empire doctrine and immortalized in *Mensagem* (Message), a kind of esoteric rewriting of Camões's *The Lusiads*. The only book of Pessoa's Portuguese poetry to see print in his lifetime, in 1934, *Mensagem* was not a mere exercise in nostalgia for Portugal's glory days during the Age of Discovery. Those glory days were to be Portugal's future as well as past destiny, and that future was now, according to the book's final line: "The Hour has come!"

When we put all the pieces together—heteronymy, the New Renaissance, the Great Poet, the Fifth Empire, mystical nationalism, and neopaganism, with Master Caeiro as its avatar—we arrive at a bizarre ultimate vision: Portugal as the hub of a cultural empire masterminded by Pessoa and radiating out to the rest of Europe, with neopaganism having replaced Catholicism, Alberto Caeiro having replaced Jesus as a new, different kind of Messiah, and perhaps Álvaro de Campos (who always dreamed of being Caesar) sitting on the emperor's throne. Pessoa, surely, did not believe in this vision in any kind of literal way. But he did believe in it poetically, metaphorically. He did stake his life and his poetic name on it. For him and in him, in his world of heteronyms, the New Renaissance, the Fifth Empire, and neopaganism existed. And according to the literary history of twentieth-century Portugal, the Great Poet (as great as, if not greater than, Camões) was indeed born in 1888.

The essence of Pessoa's nationalistic ideal, and the means for its realization, is expressed in a passage from *The Book of Disquiet* that he published in a magazine, in 1931:

> I have no social or political sentiments, and yet there is a way in which I'm highly nationalistic. My nation is the Portuguese language. It wouldn't trouble me at all if Portugal were invaded or occupied, as long as I was left in peace. But I hate with genuine hatred, with the only hatred I feel, not those who write bad Portuguese . . . , but the badly written page itself . . . .

The Book of Disquiet was credited to Bernardo Soares, a fictional bookkeeper whom Pessoa considered a "semi-heteronym," since his personality was similar, though not identical, to his own. Pessoa, writing under his own name, would never have said that he had *no* political sentiments; but for him, as for Soares, the well-written page was his passion, and the well-written page in Portuguese was his nation, his nationalism. Pessoa was in fact actively engaged in the society and the politics of his day, but it was through the written word that he took his stands, which included, in the last year of his life, 1935, a direct affront to the Salazar regime, when it passed a law banning secret societies such as Freemasonry.

And Pessoa's private life? His family relations? His loves? Pessoa maintained close ties with his relatives, living as a young man with various aunts (when he wasn't living in rented rooms), and with his mother and half sister after they returned from South Africa in 1920, following the death of Pessoa's stepfather. And Pessoa was loyal to his friends, mostly literary sorts, whom he met regularly in Lisbon's cafés. But with friends as with family, Pessoa remained resolutely private. He was sociable, witty, and in his way generous, but his inner life and emotions were channeled into his writing. He had one romantic, ultimately platonic liaison, which gave rise to a series of love letters exchanged in 1920 and again in 1929. Pessoa, especially in the second phase of the relationship, played some high literary sport, signing one of his letters as Álvaro de Campos, while in others he claimed to be going mad. The sweetheart, Ophelia Queiroz, reported when she was much older that Pessoa, whom she met in an office where they both worked, first declared his love with candle in hand and words borrowed from *Hamlet*: "O dear Ophelia, I am ill at these numbers; I have not art to reckon my groans: but that I love thee best, O most best, believe it." Perhaps it was her name that induced ultraliterary, ever-playful Pessoa to woo her in the first place.

When he was a little boy, literature was Pessoa's playground, and he never really left it. Like a lot of artists, but more so, Fernando Pessoa refused to grow up. He continued to live in a world of make-believe. Or shall we call it a world of make-literature? Believing, mere believing, bored Pessoa. Like a good artist, he harnessed his fertile imagination to make richly expressive things—his stunning poems, his well-turned prose, and his heteronymous nation, which was his greatest poetic act.

Chronology

The titles of Pessoa's works have, for the most part, been translated into English.

1887 Ricardo Reis is "born" in Porto on September 19 at 4:05 p.m.

1888 Fernando António Nogueira Pessoa is born on June 13 at the Largo de São Carlos, in Lisbon, at 3:20 p.m. He is the first child of Joaquim de Seabra Pessoa, born in Lisbon but with family roots in the Algarve, and of Maria Madalena Pinheiro Nogueira, from the island of Terceira, in the Azores.

1889 Alberto Caeiro is "born" in Lisbon on April 16 at 1:45 p.m.

1890 Álvaro de Campos is "born" on October 15 (Nietzsche's birthday) in Tavira, the Algarve, at 1:30 p.m.

1893 Pessoa's brother, Jorge, is born in January. In July his father dies from tuberculosis, and the family, which includes Dionísia, Pessoa's paternal grandmother, moves to a smaller apartment.

1894 His brother Jorge dies in January. That same month his mother meets João Miguel Rosa, a naval officer.

1895 In July Pessoa composes his first lines of verse, a quatrain addressed to his mother. On December 30 she is married, by proxy, to João Miguel Rosa, recently named Portugal's consul in Durban, largest city of the English colony of Natal.

1896 In January Pessoa and his mother embark for Durban, South Africa, where he enrolls in the Convent School. In November his mother gives birth to Henriqueta Madalena, the sibling who will be closest to Pessoa.

1899 Pessoa enrolls in Durban High School, where he receives a solid English education.

1901 His mother gives birth to Luís Miguel. After completing three years of high school in little more than two years, Pessoa passes the School Higher Examination of the University of the Cape of Good Hope. In August he sails with his family for Portugal, where they will stay for a year, mostly in Lisbon, but with trips to the Algarve (to visit the paternal relatives) and to the Azores (to visit the maternal relatives).

1902 In May the family travels to the island of Terceira, staying with Pessoa's aunt Anica (his mother's only sister). There—but also in Lisbon, before and after the trip to the Azores—Pessoa creates rather elaborate "newspapers" filled with real and invented news, jokes, riddles, and poems, all in Portuguese. The articles and other pieces are signed by various "journalists," one of whom is endowed with a biography. In July his first poem is published, in a Lisbon newspaper. In September he returns to Durban, where he enrolls in the Commercial School.

1903 His mother gives birth to João Maria. (Two daughters from her second marriage die in infancy.) In November Pessoa takes the Matriculation Examination of the University of the Cape of Good Hope and wins the Queen Victoria Prize for the best English essay from among the 899 examinees.

1904 Returns to Durban High School, where he pursues his first year of university studies. (The University of the Cape of Good Hope administers exams but does not yet offer courses.) In July he publishes, in *The Natal Mercury*, a satirical poem signed by Charles Robert Anon, the first literary alter ego with a reasonably large body of work. In December he takes the Intermediate Examination in Arts and receives the highest score in Natal. He withdraws from Durban High School.

1905 In August he returns for good to Lisbon, where he enrolls in the university-level course of Arts and Letters. During the first year he lives with his aunt Anica, who has just moved from the island of Terceira to Lisbon.

1906 Having missed the exams in July due to illness, he re-enrolls in the first year of the Arts and Letters course. He writes poetry and prose in English under the name of C. R. Anon and Alexander Search, a heteronym whose output will include close to two hundred poems and various prose pieces. In July Pessoa moves into an apartment with his family, who have arrived from Durban to spend a long holiday in Portugal.

1907 Pessoa's classes are suspended in April due to a student strike, and in May he drops out. After his family returns to Durban, in April, Pessoa lives with two maternal great-aunts, Rita and Maria. His grandmother Dionísia, who also lives with them, dies in September and leaves Pessoa, her only heir, a significant inheritance.

1909 Pessoa uses his inheritance to buy a printing press. In November he moves into his own apartment and opens the Empreza Ibis, a printing office, but it shuts down after six months and leaves him in debt. Earns a modest living as a freelancer, translating various kinds of texts and drafting letters in English and French for firms doing business abroad.

1910 On October 5, the increasingly unpopular monarchy falls and the Portuguese Republic is proclaimed.

1911 In September Pessoa's family moves from Durban to Pretoria, where his stepfather has been named consul general of Portugal.

1912 Lives once more with his aunt Anica. Publishes, in the Porto-based magazine *A Águia*, several long articles on the current state and future direction of Portuguese poetry. In October his best friend, the writer Mário de Sá-Carneiro (1890–1916), moves to Paris and a lively, literary correspondence ensues.

1913 Publishes, in *A Águia*, his first piece of creative prose, a passage from *The Book of Disquiet*, signed by his own name. Writes "Epithalamium," a long, sexually explicit poem in English.

1914 Publishes, in a magazine, his first poems as an adult. Creates, between March and June, his three main heteronyms: Alberto Caeiro, Álvaro de Campos, and Ricardo Reis. Each will sign a substantial body of poetry in Portuguese;

Campos and Reis will also be credited with several hundred pages of prose. In their writings the three heteronyms dialogue with each other and with Pessoa–himself. In November Aunt Anica moves to Switzerland with her daughter and son-in-law. For the next six years Pessoa will live in rented rooms or apartments.

1915 The magazine *Orpheu*, which introduces modernism into Portugal, is founded by a small group of poets and artists led by Pessoa and Sá-Carneiro. In the magazine's two issues, Pessoa publishes some of his major works, including a "static drama" called *The Mariner* (his only finished play), the six "intersectionist" poems of a sequence titled *Slanting Rain*, and three long poems attributed to Álvaro de Campos: "Opiary," "The Triumphal Ode," and "The Maritime Ode." Writes "Antinous," a long, homoerotic poem in English. Embarks on the translation, into Portuguese, of works by Helena Blavatsky, C. W. Leadbeater, and other Theosophical writers (six books published in 1915–16). Alberto Caeiro "dies" of tuberculosis, but poems will continue to be written in his name until 1930. In December Pessoa creates Raphael Baldaya, a heteronymous astrologer.

1916 In March he begins to write automatically, or mediumistically, receiving "communications" from Henry More (1614–1687), a certain Wardour, the Voodooist (who sometimes signs himself Joseph Balsamo, alias Count Cagliostro), and other astral spirits. During the next two years he will produce, in a childish script, several hundred pages of automatic writing, mostly in English and largely concerned with his desire to meet a woman who will "cure" him of his virginity. Mário de Sá-Carneiro commits suicide in a Paris hotel on April 26.

1917 In May submits *The Mad Fiddler*, a collection of poems, to an English publisher, who rejects the manuscript. In October publishes, in *Portugal Futurista*, Álvaro de Campos's *Ultimatum*, a manifesto that vilifies Europe's political leaders and cultural luminaries. The magazine is seized from the newsstands by the police two days later. A coup d'état in December establishes Sidónio Pais as dictator.

1918 Self-publishes two chapbooks of his English poems,

Antinous: A Poem and *35 Sonnets*. Sends copies of the books to various British journals and receives fairly positive reviews. Sidónio Pais is assassinated on December 14. Pessoa becomes a fervent post-mortem votary of the charismatic (but ineffectual) leader.

1919 In January a monarchy is proclaimed in Lisbon and Porto by military juntas organized in the preceding months. The royalist forces, quickly subdued in the south, are defeated in the north one month later. Ricardo Reis, a supporter of the monarchy, supposedly emigrates to Brazil. Pessoa actively collaborates in *Acção*, a small, right-wing journal highly critical of the Republican government. In October his stepfather dies in Pretoria. That same month Ophelia Queiroz, nineteen years old, is hired as a secretary in a firm where Pessoa sometimes works.

1920 On March 1 Pessoa writes his first love letter to Ophelia Queiroz. Besides exchanging letters, they meet each other for walks and ride the streetcar together. He breaks off with her in a letter dated November 29. In late March Pessoa's family—his mother and three grown children from her second marriage—arrives in Lisbon. His two half brothers soon leave for England, where they will study at universities in London, get married, and settle. Pessoa, his mother, and his half sister, Henriqueta, rent an apartment on the Rua Coelho da Rocha, 16, where Pessoa will reside until his death.

1921 In December Olisipo, a small company and publishing house founded by Pessoa one year earlier, publishes two books of his English poems, whose contents include "Epithalamium" (written in 1913) and a revised version of "Antinous."

1922 In May Pessoa publishes, in the magazine *Contemporânea*, a dialectical satire titled "The Anarchist Banker." In October he publishes, in the same magazine, eleven of the poems that will make up *Mensagem* (1934). In November Olisipo republishes *Canções* (Songs), a book of poems by the openly homosexual António Botto (first published in 1921).

1923 Olisipo publishes a booklet, *Sodoma Divinizada* (Sodom Deified), by Raul Leal. In response to a campaign by conservative students against the "literature of Sodom," the government bans various books deemed immoral, including *Sodoma Divinizada* and António Botto's *Canções*. Pessoa self-publishes two manifestos—one in his own name and another signed by Álvaro de Campos—criticizing the students and defending Raul Leal. In July Pessoa's sister gets married and takes their semi-invalid mother to live with her and her husband.

1924 Founds the magazine *Athena*, whose first issue (October) features twenty odes of Ricardo Reis, previously unknown to the public.

1925 The fourth and fifth (and last) issues of *Athena* present Alberto Caeiro to the public, with a total of thirty-nine poems. Pessoa's mother dies in March, and in the fall his sister and brother-in-law move back to the Rua Coelho da Rocha. In November she gives birth to Manuela Nogueira, Pessoa's only niece.

1926 Pessoa's translation of Hawthorne's *The Scarlet Letter* is serialized in the magazine *Illustração* (January 1926–February 1927), though with no mention of the translator. Pessoa and his brother-in-law found and publish six issues of the *Revista de Comércio e Contabilidade* (Business and Accounting Magazine). A coup d'état in May establishes a military dictatorship.

1927 The literary review *Presença* is founded in Coimbra. The young editors consider Pessoa, who is not especially well known, to be Portugal's most significant living writer, and they regularly publish his work throughout the rest of his life. One of the editors, João Gaspar Simões, will publish the first biography of Pessoa, in 1950. Pessoa's sister and her family move to Évora, where they will live for three years.

1928 Pessoa publishes a booklet titled *O Interregno* (The Interregnum), which defends and justifies military dictatorship as a necessary "State of Transition" in Portugal, wracked by political instability and without (according to the booklet's arguments) a "national ideal" or a tradition of strong public opinion to support a British-style, constitutional government. (In a bibliographical note dating from 1935, Pessoa will repudiate *O Interregno*.) António de Oliveira Salazar becomes the finance minister in April. In August Pessoa creates his last heteronym, the Baron of Teive, who, frustrated because of his inability to produce finished works, decides to commit suicide.

1929 Publishes, for the first time since 1913, passages from *The Book of Disquiet*, now credited to the "semiheteronym" Bernardo Soares, an assistant bookkeeper who lives and works in downtown Lisbon. (Pessoa will leave, at his death, more than five hundred passages of this work, many of which are scattered among his papers and notebooks. The first edition of *The Book of Disquiet*, compiled by scholars, will not be published until 1982.) In September Pessoa and Ophelia Queiroz rekindle their relationship, exchanging letters and occasionally seeing each other. On December 4 Pessoa writes Aleister Crowley's publisher to correct the natal horoscope published in the occult master's autobiographical *Confessions*. Crowley (1875–1947), also known as Master Therion, acknowledges the mistake and strikes up a correspondence with Pessoa.

1930 Writes his last letter to Ophelia Queiroz on January 11, but he continues to see her for another year. In September Aleister Crowley comes to Lisbon with a girlfriend, who quarrels with him after several weeks and abruptly leaves the country. Crowley, abetted by Pessoa, stages a fake suicide that receives national and international news coverage, with Pessoa being interviewed and providing false testimony. Pessoa plans and partly writes, in English, a detective novel based on the pseudo-suicide.

1931 Luís Miguel Rosa Dias, Pessoa's only nephew, is born to his half sister Henriqueta.

1932 Henriqueta and her family begin to spend long periods at a house in Estoril, where Pessoa often visits. On July 5 Salazar is appointed prime minister and becomes, in practice, a dictator.

1933 A new constitution marks the inception of Salazar's so-called Estado Novo (New State).

1934 Publishes, in the fall, *Mensagem* (Message), the only book
of his Portuguese poetry to see print in his lifetime. The book
is awarded a prize by the Secretariat of National Propaganda.

1935 Publishes, on February 4, an impassioned article against a
proposed law that would ban Freemasonry and other "secret
societies." (The National Assembly unanimously ratifies the
law in April.) In the ceremony where Pessoa's and another po-
etry prize are awarded, on February 21, Salazar's speech in-
forms writers that their creative and intellectual productions
should not only respect "certain limitations" but also obey
"certain guidelines" dictated by the Estado Novo's "moral
and patriotic principles." Pessoa, who did not attend the cer-
emony but read the speech in the newspaper, is outraged
and takes to writing poems against Salazar and his so-called
New State. The poetry of his last year also reflects, at the per-
sonal level, an increasingly felt solitude. On November 29,
beset by fever and strong abdominal pains, Pessoa is taken
to the French hospital of Lisbon. There he writes, in English,
his last words: "I know not what tomorrow will bring."
Tomorrow brings death, at around 8:30 p.m. On Decem-
ber 2 he is buried in Lisbon at the cemetery of Prazeres, where
one of the survivors of the *Orpheu* group delivers a brief
address to a small crowd.

Notes on the Selection,
Editing, and Translation

To publish Pessoa involves hard decisions, and a certain betrayal of the original. I don't mean the betrayal that comes from the incapacity of one language to replicate another—a problem faced by all translations—but the betrayal deriving from decisions the editor or translator is forced to make, since Pessoa did not. The majority of Pessoa's unpublished writings (and he published relatively little) was left in an unfinished state, which means that 1) they were not fully fleshed out, or 2) they were structurally complete but dotted with blank spaces for words or phrases the author meant to fill in later but never did, or 3) they were marked up with a number of alternate phrasings—in the margins or between the lines—for a final revision that wasn't carried out. Pessoa, an incontinent writer, was too busy turning out new poems and prose pieces to dedicate a great amount of time to revising and polishing. He did revise and polish, but he had difficulty arriving at finished products that satisfied him.

The rough and fragmentary nature of Pessoa's work occurred by default; it was not an aesthetic he cultivated. He would never have published "Salutation to Walt Whitman" or "Un Soir à Lima" as sets of more or less connectable fragments, as they appear here. There are probably poems in this collection that Pessoa, finding them imperfect and imperfectible, would have eliminated, had he ever gotten around to preparing his work for publication. And it's impossible to know exactly how poem XXXIII in The Keeper of Sheep would have ended, had its author chosen from among the six versions for the concluding line that litter the manuscript. They're not litter, of course, but only one version can appear in the body of the text; the rest must be relegated to notes. Hesitancy and multiplicity, which marked Pessoa's psychological existence, also permeate the written universe he left to posterity.

To make matters even more interesting (or "complicated," which to Pessoa's way of thinking was a synonym for "interesting"), the handwriting on the manuscripts sometimes verges on the hieroglyphic. There are lines from "Salutation to Walt Whitman," for example, that no one has yet managed to decipher. In the first large-scale edition of Pessoa's poetry, initiated in the 1940s, misreadings of single words and entire sentences were frequent, and the "Salutation," besides suffering from faulty transcriptions, was presented as a finished poem, for which only a handful of its more than twenty pieces were stitched together to form a false whole that wasn't even logically coherent, let alone editorially honest. Other poems, such as "I want to be free and insincere" (p. 308), were missing one or more stanzas, or the stanzas were out of order.

Greatly improved editions of Pessoa's poetry have been made during the last fifteen years. Since even these have occasional errors of transcription, I have consulted all the available manuscripts of the poems contained in the present volume except for those published by the author himself. Divergent readings are accounted for in the endnotes. Where a manuscript contains more than one version of a word or phrase, I have preferred whichever seemed to me to work best; the other versions are referred to as "variants," and the most significant of these are recorded in the endnotes.

Where the original poem rhymes (generally the case of poems signed by Pessoa himself, occasionally the case of Álvaro de Campos, and almost never the case of Alberto Caeiro or Ricardo Reis), my translation sometimes follows suit, usually in a modified scheme—e.g., one rhyme per four-line stanza instead of two—and with recourse to slant rhymes. Curiously enough, Pessoa's translations of English and American poems into Portuguese scrupulously conserved the rhyme schemes of the original, but when he translated a few stanzas of Álvaro de Campos's "Opiary" into English, he dispensed with rhyme entirely. It's such a waggish poem that I feel it needs rhyme, but I employed a simpler *abcb* scheme instead of the *abba* pattern of the original.

I have generally respected Pessoa's apparently erratic use of uppercase letters: *gods* in one poem and *Gods* in another, or *universe* and *Universe* occurring in the same poem ("Salutation"). The date of a given poem may refer to its initial composition or to a later revision, with months or sometimes years separating the two. Conjectural dates, based on manuscript and other evidence, appear in brackets, with a question mark indicating that the conjecture is dicey. Poems have been ordered chronologically, as far as possible, except in the case of *The Keeper of Sheep* and *Message*, which the author structured according to other criteria, and in the case of *Faust*, for which very few dates exist.

Fernando Pessoa & Co.—Selected Poems, published by Grove Press in 1998, included poems that for the most part had never before appeared in a widely circulating translation into English. There was very little crossover between that volume and the Edwin Honig / Susan Brown *Poems of Pessoa* (1986). My objective in the present *Selected* was to avoid crossover with myself. Though this contains a considerably larger number of poems, it is not an enlargement on *Fernando Pessoa & Co.* In fact only four short poems have here been reprinted (with the gracious permission of Grove Press). As in that earlier work, many of the poems offered in this volume have not heretofore been translated into English, and some have only recently come to light in Portuguese. *"Un Soir à Lima,"* Pessoa's moving and highly autobiographical swan song, remained unpublished in Portuguese until the year 2000, and the second and third of the "Uncollected Poems" of Caeiro (pp. 56–57), as well as a dozen or so of the shorter "orthonymic" poems, were first published only within the last five years.

The reader, in approaching the poems written directly in English, needs to make a slight leap. Pessoa's English, as explained in the Introduction, was fluent but bookish, and his poetic models were Shelley and other English Romantics, or, in the case of his sonnets, Shakespeare.

This book owes much to Manuela Rocha for clarifying my understanding of certain passages in the Portuguese, and to Amanda Booth and Martin Earl, who both spent many hours reading my translations and making suggestions to improve the phrasing in English. Many other friends and acquaintances—too numerous to name—have encouraged and helped me in large and small, practical and "spiritual" ways. If you are one of them, please accept my deeply felt thanks.

ONE FURTHER NOTE

Several of the poems in this selection mention floor numbers for apartments. "First floor," in Portugal as in most of the rest of Europe, corresponds to what is called the second floor in the United States, Canada, and some other countries, "second floor" corresponds to the third floor, and so forth. This revised edition respects the Portuguese/European system of numbering floors.

R. Z.

A Little Larger Than the Entire Universe

SELECTED POEMS

IN LIEU OF AN
AUTHOR'S PREFACE

*Fernando Pessoa's writings belong to two categories of
works, which we may call orthonymous and heteronymous.
We cannot call them autonymous and pseudonymous, for
that's not in fact what they are. Pseudonymous works are
by the author in his own person, except in the name he
signs; heteronymous works are by the author outside his
own person. They proceed from a full-fledged individual
created by him, like the lines spoken by a character in a
drama he might write.*

*The heteronymous works of Fernando Pessoa have been
produced by (so far) three people's names—Alberto Caeiro,
Ricardo Reis, and Álvaro de Campos. These individuals
should be considered distinct from their author. Each one
forms a kind of drama, and all of them together form
another drama. Alberto Caeiro, deeming himself born
in 1889 and dying in 1915, wrote poems with a definite
orientation. The other two were his disciples, each originating
(as disciples) from a different aspect of that orientation.*

*Ricardo Reis, who considers himself born in 1887,
isolated and stylized the intellectual and pagan aspect
of Caeiro's work. Álvaro de Campos, born in 1890,
isolated the work's (so to speak) emotive side, which he
designated as "sensationist" and which—in combination
with other, lesser influences, most notably that of Walt
Whitman—gave rise to various compositions. These are
generally of a scandalous and irritating nature, particularly
for Fernando Pessoa, who in any case has no choice but to
write and publish them, however much he disagrees with
them. The works of these three poets form, as I've said, a
dramatic ensemble, and the intellectual interaction of their
personalities as well as their actual personal relationships*

*have been duly studied. All of this will go into biographies
to be accompanied, when published, by astrological charts
and perhaps photographs. It's a drama divided into people
instead of into acts.*

*(If these three individuals are more or less real than
Fernando Pessoa himself is a metaphysical problem that the
latter—not privy to the secret of the Gods and therefore
ignorant of what reality is—will never be able to solve.)*

(FROM A "BIBLIOGRAPHICAL SUMMARY" DRAWN UP BY
PESSOA AND PUBLISHED IN 1928)

*A few more notes on this subject. . . . I see before me, in the
colorless but real space of dreams, the faces and gestures of
Caeiro, Ricardo Reis and Álvaro de Campos. I gave them
their ages and fashioned their lives. Ricardo Reis was born
in 1887 (I don't remember the month and day, but I have
them somewhere) in Porto. He's a doctor and presently
lives in Brazil. Alberto Caeiro was born in 1889 and died in
1915. He was born in Lisbon but spent most of his life in
the country. He had no profession and practically no
schooling. Álvaro de Campos was born in Tavira, on
October 15, 1890. . . . Campos, as you know, is a naval
engineer (he studied in Glasgow) but is currently living in
Lisbon and not working. Caeiro was of medium height,
and although his health was indeed fragile (he died of
tuberculosis), he seemed less frail than he was. Ricardo Reis
is a wee bit shorter, stronger, but lean. Álvaro de Campos is
tall (5 ft. 9 in., an inch taller than me), slim, and a bit
prone to stoop. All are clean-shaven—Caeiro fair, with a
pale complexion and blue eyes; Reis somewhat dark-
skinned; Campos neither pale nor dark, vaguely
corresponding to the Portuguese Jewish type, but with
smooth hair that's usually parted on one side, and a
monocle. Caeiro, as I've said, had almost no education—
just primary school. His mother and father died when he
was young, and he stayed on at home, living off a small
income from family properties. He lived with an elderly
great-aunt. Ricardo Reis, educated in a Jesuit high school,
is, as I've mentioned, a physician; he has been living in
Brazil since 1919, having gone into voluntary exile because*

of his monarchist sympathies. He is a formally trained Latinist, and a self-taught semi-Hellenist. Álvaro de Campos, after a normal high school education, was sent to Scotland to study engineering, first mechanical and then naval. During some holidays he made a voyage to the Far East, which gave rise to his poem "Opiary." An uncle who was a priest from the Beira region taught him Latin.

How do I write in the names of these three? Caeiro, through sheer and unexpected inspiration, without knowing or even suspecting that I'm going to write in his name. Ricardo Reis, after an abstract meditation that suddenly takes concrete shape in an ode. Campos, when I feel a sudden impulse to write and don't know what.

(FROM A LETTER DATED 13 JANUARY 1935)

ALBERTO CAEIRO

I'm not a materialist or a deist or anything else. I'm a man who one day opened the window and discovered this crucial thing: Nature exists. I saw that the trees, the rivers and the stones are things that truly exist. No one had ever thought about this.

I don't pretend to be anything more than the greatest poet in the world. I made the greatest discovery worth making, next to which all other discoveries are games of stupid children. I noticed the Universe. The Greeks, with all their visual acuity, didn't do as much.

(FROM AN "INTERVIEW" WITH ALBERTO CAEIRO
CONDUCTED IN VIGO)

from

THE KEEPER OF SHEEP

II

My gaze is clear like a sunflower.
It is my custom to walk the roads
Looking right and left
And sometimes looking behind me,
And what I see at each moment
Is what I never saw before,
And I'm very good at noticing things.
I'm capable of feeling the same wonder
A newborn child would feel
If he noticed that he'd really and truly been born.
I feel at each moment that I've just been born
Into a completely new world . . .

I believe in the world as in a daisy,
Because I see it. But I don't think about it,
Because to think is to not understand.
The world wasn't made for us to think about it
(To think is to have eyes that aren't well)
But to look at it and to be in agreement.

I have no philosophy, I have senses . . .
If I speak of Nature it's not because I know what it is
But because I love it, and for that very reason,
Because those who love never know what they love
Or why they love, or what love is.

To love is the supreme innocence,
And the sum of innocence is to not think . . .

8 MARCH 1914

IV

This afternoon a thunderstorm
Rolled down from the slopes of the sky
Like a huge boulder . . .

As when someone shakes a tablecloth
From out of a high window,
And the crumbs, because they fall together,
Make a sound when they fall,
The rain swished down from the sky
And darkened the roads . . .

As the bolts of lightning jostled space
And shook the air
Like a large head saying no,
I don't know why (for I wasn't afraid),
But I felt like praying to St. Barbara
As if I were somebody's old aunt . . .

Ah, by praying to St. Barbara
I'd feel even simpler
Than I think I am . . .
I'd feel common and domestic,
As if I'd lived my whole life
Peacefully, like the garden wall,
Having ideas and feelings the same way
A flower has scent and color . . .

I felt like someone who could believe in St. Barbara . . .
Ah, to be able to believe in St. Barbara!

(Do those who believe in St. Barbara
Think she's like us and visible?
Or what then do they think of her?)

(What a sham! What do the flowers,
The trees and the sheep know
About St. Barbara? . . . The branch of a tree,
If it could think, would never
Invent saints or angels . . .
It might think that the sun
Illuminates and that thunder
Is a sudden noise
That begins with light . . .
Ah, how even the simplest men
Are sick and confused and stupid
Next to the sheer simplicity
And healthy existence
Of plants and trees!)

And thinking about all this,
I became less happy again . . .
I became gloomy and out of sorts and sullen
Like a day when a thunderstorm threatens all day
And by nightfall it still hasn't struck.

VI

To think about God is to disobey God,
Since God wanted us not to know him,
Which is why he didn't reveal himself to us . . .

Let's be simple and calm,
Like the trees and streams,
And God will love us, making us
Us even as the trees are trees
And the streams are streams,
And will give us greenness in the spring, which is its season,
And a river to go to when we end . . .
And he'll give us nothing more, since to give us more would
    make us less us.

VII

From my village I see as much of the universe as can be seen
    from the earth,
And so my village is as large as any town,
For I am the size of what I see
And not the size of my height . . .

In the cities life is smaller
Than here in my house on top of this hill.
The big buildings of cities lock up the view,
They hide the horizon, pulling our gaze far away from the
    open sky.
They make us small, for they take away all the vastness our
    eyes can see,
And they make us poor, for our only wealth is seeing.

VIII

One midday in late spring
I had a dream that was like a photograph.
I saw Jesus Christ come down to earth.

He came down a hillside
As a child again,
Running and tumbling through the grass,
Pulling up flowers to throw them back down,
And laughing loud enough to be heard far away.

He had run away from heaven.
He was too much like us to fake
Being the second person of the Trinity.
In heaven everything was false and in disagreement
With flowers and trees and stones.
In heaven he always had to be serious
And now and then had to become man again
And get up on the cross, and be forever dying
With a crown full of thorns on his head,
A huge nail piercing his feet,
And even a rag around his waist
Like on black Africans in illustrated books.
He wasn't even allowed a mother and father
Like other children.
His father was two different people—
An old man named Joseph who was a carpenter
And who wasn't his father,
And an idiotic dove:

The only ugly dove in the world,
Because it wasn't of the world and wasn't a dove.
And his mother gave birth to him without ever having loved.
She wasn't a woman: she was a suitcase
In which he was sent from heaven.
And they wanted him, born only of a mother
And with no father he could love and honor,
To preach goodness and justice!

One day when God was sleeping
And the Holy Spirit was flying about,
He went to the chest of miracles and stole three.
He used the first to make everyone blind to his escape.
He used the second to make himself eternally human and a
    child.
He used the third to make an eternally crucified Christ
Whom he left nailed to the cross that's in heaven
And serves as the model for all the others.
Then he fled to the sun
And descended on the first ray he could catch.

Today he lives with me in my village.
He's a simple child with a pretty laugh.
He wipes his nose with his right arm,
Splashes about in puddles,
Plucks flowers and loves them and forgets them.
He throws stones at the donkeys,
Steals fruit from the orchards,
And runs away crying and screaming from the dogs.
And because he knows that they don't like it
And that everyone thinks it's funny,
He runs after the girls
Who walk in groups along the roads
Carrying jugs on their heads,
And he lifts up their skirts.

He taught me all I know.
He taught me to look at things.

He shows me all the things there are in flowers.
He shows me how curious stones are
When we hold them in our hand
And look at them slowly.

He speaks very badly of God.
He says God is a sick and stupid old man
Who's always swearing
And spitting on the floor.
The Virgin Mary spends the afternoons of eternity knitting.
And the Holy Spirit scratches himself with his beak
And perches on the chairs, getting them dirty.
Everything in heaven is stupid, just like the Catholic Church.
He says God understands nothing
About the things he created.
"If he created them, which I doubt," he says.
"God claims, for instance, that all beings sing his glory,
But beings don't sing anything.
If they sang, they'd be singers.
Beings exist, that's all,
Which is why they're called beings."

And then, tired of speaking badly about God,
The little boy Jesus falls asleep in my lap
And I carry him home in my arms.

. . . .

He lives with me in my house, halfway up the hill.
He's the Eternal Child, the god who was missing.
He's completely natural in his humanity.
He smiles and plays in his divinity.
And that's how I know beyond all doubt
That he's truly the little boy Jesus.

And this child who's so human he's divine
Is my daily life as a poet.
It's because he's always with me that I'm always a poet

And that my briefest glance
Fills me with feeling,
And the faintest sound, whatever it is,
Seems to be speaking to me.

The New Child who lives where I live
Gives one hand to me
And the other to everything that exists,
And so the three of us go along whatever road we find,
Leaping and singing and laughing
And enjoying our shared secret
Of knowing that in all the world
There is no mystery
And that everything is worthwhile.

The Eternal Child is always at my side.
The direction of my gaze is his pointing finger.
My happy listening to each and every sound
Is him playfully tickling my ears.

We get along so well with each other
In the company of everything
That we never even think of each other,
But the two of us live together,
Intimately connected
Like the right hand and the left.

At day's end we play jacks
On the doorstep of the house,
With the solemnity befitting a god and a poet
And as if each jack
Were an entire universe,
Such that it would be a great peril
To let one fall to the ground.

Then I tell him stories about purely human matters
And he smiles, because it's all so incredible.

He laughs at kings and those who aren't kings,
And feels sorry when he hears about wars,
And about commerce, and about ships
That are finally just smoke hovering over the high seas.
For he knows that all of this lacks the truth
Which is in a flower when it flowers
And with the sunlight when it dapples
The hills and valleys
Or makes our eyes smart before whitewashed walls.

Then he falls asleep and I put him to bed.
I carry him in my arms into the house
And lay him down, removing his clothes
Slowly and as if following a very pure
And maternal ritual until he's naked.

He sleeps inside my soul
And sometimes wakes up in the night
And plays with my dreams.
He flips some of them over in the air,
Piles some on top of others,
And claps his hands all by himself,
Smiling at my slumber.

. . . .

When I die, my son,
Let me be the child, the little one.
Pick me up in your arms
And carry me into your house.
Undress my tired and human self
And tuck me into your bed.
If I wake up, tell me stories
So that I'll fall back asleep.
And give me your dreams to play with
Until the dawning of that day
You know will dawn.

. . . .

This is the story of my little boy Jesus,
And is there any good reason
Why it shouldn't be truer
Than everything philosophers think
And all that religions teach?

IX

I'm a keeper of sheep.
The sheep are my thoughts
And each thought a sensation.
I think with my eyes and my ears
And with my hands and feet
And with my nose and mouth.

To think a flower is to see and smell it,
And to eat a fruit is to know its meaning.

That is why on a hot day
When I enjoy it so much I feel sad,
And I lie down in the grass
And close my warm eyes,
Then I feel my whole body lying down in reality,
I know the truth, and I'm happy.

XIII

Lightly, lightly, very lightly
A very light wind passes,
And it goes away just as lightly,
And I don't know what I'm thinking,
Nor do I wish to know.

XIV

I don't worry about rhyme. Two trees,
One next to the other, are rarely identical.
I think and write the way flowers have color,
But how I express myself is less perfect,
For I lack the divine simplicity
Of being only my outer self.

I look and I am moved,
I am moved the way water flows when the ground slopes,
And my poetry is natural like the stirring of the wind . . .

7 MARCH 1914

XVI

If only my life were an oxcart
That creaks down the road in the morning,
Very early, and returns by the same road
To where it came from in the evening . . .

I wouldn't have to have hopes, just wheels . . .
My old age wouldn't have wrinkles or white hair . . .
When I was of no more use, my wheels would be removed
And I'd end up in a gully, broken and overturned.

Or I'd be made into something different
And I wouldn't know what I'd been made into . . .
But I'm not an oxcart, I'm different.
But exactly how I'm different no one would ever tell me.

4 MARCH 1914

XVII

SALAD

What a medley of Nature fills my plate!
My sisters the plants,
The companions of springs, the saints
No one prays to . . .

And they're cut and brought to our table,
And in the hotels the noisy guests
Arrive with their strapped-up blankets
And casually order "Salad,"

Without thinking that they're requiring Mother Earth
To give her freshness and her first-born children,
Her very first green words,
The first living and gleaming things
That Noah saw
When the waters subsided and the hilltops emerged
All drenched and green,
And in the sky where the dove appeared
The rainbow came into view . . .

7 MARCH 1914

XXI

If I could sink my teeth into the whole earth
And actually taste it,
I'd be happier for a moment . . .
But I don't always want to be happy.
To be unhappy now and then
Is part of being natural.
Not all days are sunny,
And when rain is scarce, we pray for it.
And so I take unhappiness with happiness
Naturally, just as I don't marvel
That there are mountains and plains
And that there are rocks and grass . . .

What matters is to be natural and calm
In happiness and in unhappiness,
To feel as if feeling were seeing,
To think as if thinking were walking,
And to remember, when death comes, that each day dies,
And the sunset is beautiful, and so is the night that
    remains . . .
And if that's how it is, it's because that's how it is . . .

7 MARCH 1914

XXVI

Sometimes, on days of perfect and exact light,
When things are as real as they can possibly be,
I slowly ask myself
Why I even bother to attribute
Beauty to things.

Does a flower really have beauty?
Does a fruit really have beauty?
No: they have only color and form
And existence.
Beauty is the name of something that doesn't exist
But that I give to things in exchange for the pleasure they
    give me.
It means nothing.
So why do I say about things: they're beautiful?

Yes, even I, who live only off living,
Am unwittingly visited by the lies of men
Concerning things,
Concerning things that simply exist.

How hard to be just what we are and see nothing but the
    visible!

11 MARCH 1914

XXVII

Only Nature is divine, and she is not divine . . .

If I sometimes speak of her as a person
It's because I can only speak of her by using the language
of men,
Which imposes names on things
And gives them personality.

But things have no name or personality:
They just are, and the sky is vast, the earth wide,
And our heart the size of a closed fist . . .

Blessed am I for all I don't know.
That's all I truly am . . .
I enjoy it all as one who knows that the sun exists.

XXVIII

Today I read nearly two pages
In the book of a mystic poet,
And I laughed as if I'd cried a lot.

Mystic poets are sick philosophers,
And philosophers are lunatics.
Because mystic poets say that flowers feel
And that stones have souls
And that rivers are filled with rapture in the moonlight.

But flowers, if they felt, wouldn't be flowers,
They would be people;
And if stones had souls, they would be living things, not
    stones;
And if rivers were filled with rapture in the moonlight,
Those rivers would be sick people.

Only one who doesn't know what flowers and stones and
    rivers are
Can talk about their feelings.
Those who talk about the soul of stones, of flowers and of
    rivers
Are talking about themselves and their false notions.
Thank God that stones are just stones,
And rivers nothing but rivers,
And flowers merely flowers.

As for me, I write the prose of my verses
And am satisfied,
Because I know I understand Nature on the outside,
And I don't understand it on the inside,
Because Nature has no inside.
If it did, it wouldn't be Nature.

XXX

If you want me to have a mysticism, then fine, I have one.
I'm a mystic, but only with my body.
My soul is simple and doesn't think.

My mysticism is not wanting to know.
It's living and not thinking about it.

I don't know what Nature is: I sing it.
I live on top of a hill
In a solitary, whitewashed house,
And that is my definition.

XXXI

If sometimes I say that flowers smile
And if I should say that rivers sing,
It's not because I think there are smiles in flowers
And songs in the rivers' flowing . . .
It's so I can help misguided people
Feel the truly real existence of flowers and rivers.

Since I write for them to read me, I sometimes stoop
To the stupidity of their senses . . .
It isn't right, but I excuse myself,
Because I don't seriously accept my behavior,
Because I've only taken on this odious role, an interpreter of
    Nature,
For the sake of those who don't grasp its language,
Which is no language at all.

XXXIII

Poor flowers in the flower beds of manicured gardens.
They look like they're afraid of the police . . .
But they're so true that they bloom in the same way
And have the same ancient coloring
They had in their wild state for the first gaze of the first
    man,
Who was startled by the sight of them and touched them
    lightly
So that he would see them with his fingers too.

XXXIV

I find it so natural not to think
That I sometimes start laughing, all by myself,
About I don't know quite what, but it has to do
With there being people who think . . .

What does my wall think about my shadow?
Sometimes I wonder about this until I realize
I'm wondering about things . . .
And then I feel annoyed and out of sorts with myself,
As if I'd realized my foot was asleep . . .

What does one thing think about another?
Nothing thinks anything.
Is the earth aware of the stones and plants it contains?
If it were, it would be a person,
And if it were a person, it would have a person's nature, it
    wouldn't be the earth.
But what does all this matter to me?
If I thought about these things,
I would stop seeing the trees and plants
And would stop seeing the Earth,
Seeing nothing but my thoughts . . .
I would grow sad and remain in the dark.
The way I am, without thinking, I have the Earth and the Sky.

XXXV

The moonlight seen through the tall branches
Is more, say all the poets,
Than the moonlight seen through the tall branches.

But for me, oblivious to what I think,
The moonlight seen through the tall branches,
Besides its being
The moonlight seen through the tall branches,
Is its not being more
Than the moonlight seen through the tall branches.

XXXVI

And there are poets who are artists
And they fashion their verses
Like a carpenter his boards! . . .

How sad not to know how to blossom!
To have to place verse upon verse, as if building a wall,
Making sure each one is right, and taking it away if it
    isn't! . . .
When the only true house is the whole Earth,
Which varies and is always right and is always the same.

I think about this not as one who thinks but as one who
    doesn't,
And I look at the flowers and smile . . .
I don't know if they understand me
Or if I understand them,
But I know the truth is in them and in me
And in our common divinity
Of letting go and living right here on the Earth
And contentedly cuddling up in the Seasons
And letting the wind gently sing us to sleep
And having no dreams in our slumber.

XLI

On certain summer days, when the dusk is falling,
Even if there's no breeze, it seems
For a moment that a light breeze is blowing . . .
But the trees remain still
In their leaves' every aspect.
Our senses had an illusion—
The illusion of what, in that moment, would please them . . .

Ah, our senses, such sick observers and listeners!
Were we as we should be,
We wouldn't need any illusions . . .
It would be enough for us to feel with clarity and life,
Without even noticing what the senses are for . . .

But thank God there's imperfection in the World,
Since imperfection is a thing,
And the existence of mistaken people is original,
And the existence of sick people makes the world
    bigger.
If there were no imperfection, there would be one less thing,
And there should be many things
So that we will have a lot to see and hear
For as long as our eyes and ears remain open . . .

7 MAY 1914

XLIII

Better the flight of the bird that passes and leaves no trace
Than the passage of the animal, recorded in the ground.
The bird passes and is forgotten, which is how it should be.
The animal, no longer there and so of no further use,
Uselessly shows it was there.

Remembrance is a betrayal of Nature,
Because yesterday's Nature isn't Nature.
What was is nothing, and to remember is not to see.

Pass by, bird, pass, and teach me to pass!

7 MAY 1914

XLV

A row of trees in the distance, toward the slope . . .
But what is a row of trees? There are just trees.
"Row" and the plural "trees" are names, not things.

Unhappy human beings, who put everything in order,
Draw lines from thing to thing,
Place labels with names on absolutely real trees,
And plot parallels of latitude and longitude
On the innocent earth itself, which is so much greener and full
    of flowers!

7 MAY 1914

XLVI

In this way or that way,
As it may happen or not happen,
Sometimes succeeding in saying what I think
And at other times saying it badly and with digressions,
I keep writing my poems, inadvertently,
As if writing were not something requiring action,
As if writing were something that happens to me
In the same way that the sun reaches me from outside.

I try to say what I feel
Without thinking about what I feel.
I try to place words right next to my idea
So that I won't need a corridor
Of thought leading to words.

I don't always manage to feel what I know I should feel.
Only very slowly does my thought swim across the river,
Weighed down as it is by the suit people forced it to wear.

I try to shed what I've learned,
I try to forget the way I was taught to remember,
To scrape off the paint that was painted on my senses,
To uncrate my true emotions,
To step out of all my wrapping and be myself—not Alberto
    Caeiro
But a human animal created by Nature.

That's how I write, wanting to feel Nature not even as a man
But merely as someone who feels Nature.
That's how I write, sometimes well, sometimes badly,
Sometimes saying just what I want to say, sometimes getting
    it wrong,
Falling down one moment and getting up the next,
But always continuing on my way like a stubborn blind
    man.

Even so, I'm somebody.
I'm the Discoverer of Nature.
I'm the Argonaut of true sensations.
I bring to the Universe a new Universe,
Because I bring to the Universe its own self.

This is what I feel and write,
Perfectly aware and clearly seeing
That it's five o'clock in the morning
And that the sun, although it still hasn't raised its face
Over the wall of the horizon,
Is already showing the tips of its fingers
Gripping the top of the wall
Of the horizon sprinkled with low hills.

10 MAY 1914

XLVIII

From the highest window of my house
I wave farewell with a white handkerchief
To my poems going out to humanity.

And I'm neither happy nor sad.
That is the fate of poems.
I wrote them and must show them to everyone
Because I cannot do otherwise,
Even as the flower can't hide its color,
Nor the river hide its flowing,
Nor the tree hide the fruit it bears.

There they go, already far away, as if in the stagecoach,
And I can't help but feel regret
Like a pain in my body.

Who knows who might read them?
Who knows into what hands they'll fall?

A flower, I was plucked by my fate to be seen.
A tree, my fruit was picked to be eaten.
A river, my water's fate was to flow out of me.
I submit and feel almost happy,
Almost happy like a man tired of being sad.

Go, go away from me!
The tree passes and is scattered throughout Nature.

The flower wilts and its dust lasts forever.
The river flows into the sea and its water is forever the water
   that was its own.

I pass and I remain, like the Universe.

XLIX

I go inside and shut the window.
The lamp is brought and I'm told good night.
And my voice contentedly says good night.
May this be my life, now and always:
The day bright with sunshine, or gentle with rain,
Or stormy as if the world were ending,
The evening gentle and my eyes attentive
To the people passing by my window,
With my last friendly gaze going to the peaceful trees,
And then, window shut and the lamp lit,
Without reading or sleeping and thinking of nothing,
To feel life flowing through me like a river between its banks,
And outside a great silence like a god who is sleeping.

from

THE SHEPHERD IN LOVE

The moon is high up in the sky and it's spring.
I think of you and within myself I'm complete.

A light breeze comes to me from across the hazy fields.
I think of you and whisper your name. I'm not I: I'm happy.

Tomorrow you'll come and walk with me and pick flowers in
the fields.
And I'll walk with you in the fields watching you pick
flowers.

I already see you tomorrow picking flowers with me in the
fields,
But when you come tomorrow and really walk with me and
pick flowers,
For me it will be a joy and a novelty.

6 JULY 1914

Now that I feel love,
I'm interested in fragrances.
It never used to interest me that flowers have smell.
Now I feel their fragrance as if I were seeing something new.
I know they smelled before, just as I know I existed.
These are things we know outwardly.
But now I know with the breathing at the back of my head.
Now flowers have a delicious taste I can smell.
Now I sometimes wake up and smell before I see.

23 JULY 1930

Love is a company.
I no longer know how to walk the roads alone,
For I'm no longer able to walk alone.
A visible thought makes me walk faster
And see less, and at the same time enjoy all I see.
Even her absence is something that's with me.
And I like her so much I don't know how to desire her.
If I don't see her, I imagine her and am strong like the tall
    trees.
But if I see her I tremble, I don't know what's happened to
    what I feel in her absence.
The whole of me is like a force that abandons me.
All of reality looks at me like a sunflower with her face in the
    middle.

10 JULY 1930

Unable to sleep, I spent the whole night seeing her figure all
    by itself
And seeing it always in ways different from when I see her in
    person.
I fashion thoughts from my memory of how she is when she
    talks to me,
And in each thought she's a variation on her likeness.
To love is to think.
And from thinking of her so much, I almost forget to feel.
I don't really know what I want, even from her, and she's all I
    think of.
My mental distraction is as large as life.
When I feel like being with her,
I almost prefer not being with her,
So as not to have to leave her afterwards.
And I prefer thinking about her, because I'm a little afraid of
    her as she really is.
I don't really know what I want, and I don't even want to
    know what I want.
All I want is to think her.
I don't ask anything of anyone, not even of her, except to let
    me think.

10 JULY 1930

from
UNCOLLECTED POEMS

Beyond the bend in the road
There may be a well, and there may be a castle,
And there may be just more road.
I don't know and don't ask.
As long as I'm on the road that's before the bend
I look only at the road before the bend,
Because the road before the bend is all I can see.
It would do me no good to look anywhere else
Or at what I can't see.
Let's pay attention only to where we are.
There's enough beauty in being here and not somewhere else.
If there are people beyond the bend in the road,
Let them worry about what's beyond the bend in the road.
That, for them, is the road.
If we're to arrive there, when we arrive there we'll know.
For now we know only that we're not there.
Here there's just the road before the bend, and before the bend
There's the road without any bend.

[1914]

To clean and tidy up Matter . . .
To put back all the things people cluttered up
Because they didn't understand what they were for . . .
To straighten, like a diligent housekeeper of Reality,
The curtains on the windows of Feeling
And the mats before the doors of Perception . . .
To sweep the rooms of observation
And to dust off simple ideas . . .
That's my life, verse by verse.

17 SEPTEMBER 1914

What's my life worth? In the end (I don't know what end)
One man says: "I earned three hundred thousand dollars."
Another man says: "I enjoyed three thousand days of glory."
Yet another says: "I had a clear conscience and that's enough."
And I, should somebody ask what I did,
Will say: "Nothing except look at things,
Which is why I have the whole Universe in my pocket."
And if God should ask: "And what did you see in things?"
I'll answer: "Just the things themselves. That's all you put
    there."
And God, who after all is savvy, will make me into a new kind
    of saint.

17 SEPTEMBER 1914

The astonishing reality of things
Is my discovery every day.
Each thing is what it is,
And it's hard to explain to someone how happy this
    makes me,
And how much this suffices me.

All it takes to be complete is to exist.

I've written quite a few poems,
I'll no doubt write many more,
And this is what every poem of mine says,
And all my poems are different,
Because each thing that exists is a different way of saying this.

Sometimes I pause to look at a stone.
I don't pause to think about whether it exists.
I don't get sidetracked, calling it my sister.
I like it for being a stone,
I like it because it feels nothing,
I like it because it's not related to me in any way.

At other times I hear the wind blow,
And I feel that it was worth being born just to hear the wind
    blow.

I don't know what people will think when they read this,
But I feel it must be right since I think it without any effort

Or any idea of what people who hear me will think,
Because I think it without thoughts,
Because I say it the way my words say it.

I was once called a materialist poet,
And it surprised me, for I didn't think
I could be called anything.
I'm not even a poet: I see.
If what I write has any value, the value isn't mine,
It belongs to my poems.
All this is absolutely independent of my will.

7 NOVEMBER 1915

When spring arrives,
If I'm already dead,
The flowers will flower in the same way
And the trees will not be less green than last spring.
Reality doesn't need me.

It makes me enormously happy
To think that my death is of no importance whatsoever.

If I knew that I would die tomorrow
And that spring was the day after tomorrow,
I would die happy, because spring was the day after
    tomorrow.
If that is its time, why should it come at some other time?
I like everything to be real and to be right,
And I like it that way because that's how it would be even if
    I didn't like it.
And so, if I die now, I'll die happy,
Because everything is real and everything is right.

You can pray in Latin over my coffin, if you like.
If you like, you can sing and dance in a circle around it.
I have no preferences for when I can no longer have
    preferences.
What will be, when it is, is what it will be when it is.

7 NOVEMBER 1915

If, after I die, someone wants to write my biography,
There's nothing simpler.
It has just two dates—the day I was born and the day I died.
Between the two, all the days are mine.

I'm easy to define.
I saw as if damned to see.
I loved things without any sentimentality.
I never had a desire I couldn't satisfy, because I was never
    blind.
Even hearing was never more for me than an accompaniment
    to seeing.
I understood that things are real and all of them different
    from each other.
I understood this with my eyes, never with my mind.
To understand this with my mind would be to find them all
    alike.

One day, like a child, I suddenly got tired.
I closed my eyes and fell asleep.

Besides all that, I was Nature's only poet.

8 NOVEMBER 1915

I don't know how anyone can think a sunset is sad,
Unless it's because a sunset isn't a sunrise.
But if it's a sunset, how could it ever be a sunrise?

8 NOVEMBER 1915

You speak of civilization and how it shouldn't exist,
At least not in its present form.
You say that everyone, or almost everyone, suffers
From human life being organized in this way.
You say that if things were different, people would suffer less.
You say things would be better if they were how you want
    them.
I hear you and don't listen.
Why would I want to listen to you?
I'd learn nothing by listening to you.
If things were different, they'd be different: that's all.
If things were how you want them, they'd be how you want
    them, fine.
Too bad for you and for all who spend life
Trying to invent the machine for producing happiness!

Today someone read me St. Francis of Assisi.
I listened and couldn't believe my ears.
How could a man who was so fond of things
 Never have looked at them or understood what they were?

Why call water my sister if water isn't my sister?
To feel it better?
I feel it better by drinking it than by calling it something—
Sister, or mother, or daughter.
Water is beautiful because it's water.
If I call it my sister,
I can see, even as I call it that, that it's not my sister
And that it's best to call it water, since that's what it is,
Or, better yet, not to call it anything
But to drink it, to feel it on my wrists, and to look at it,
Without any names.

21 MAY 1917

I see in the distance a ship on the Tagus . . .
It's sailing downriver indifferently.
Not indifferently because it ignores me
And I don't care, but indifferently
Because it has no meaning
Outside the exclusively shippish fact
Of sailing downriver without permission from metaphysics . . .
Downriver toward the reality of sea.

1 OCTOBER 1917

When it's cold in the season for cold, to me it feels pleasant,
Since, suited as I am to how things exist,
What's natural is what's pleasant just because it's natural.

I accept life's hardships because they're destiny,
As I accept the harsh cold in the dead of winter—
Calmly and without complaint, as one who simply accepts,
And finds joy in the fact of accepting,
In the sublimely scientific and difficult fact of accepting the
    inevitably natural.

Aren't the illnesses I have and the adversity I experience
Just the winter of my life and person?
An erratic winter, whose laws of appearing are unknown to me
But that exists for me by the same sublime fatality,
The same external and inevitable reality,
As the earth's heat in high summer
And the earth's cold in the depths of winter.

I accept because it's my nature to accept.
Like everyone, I was born subject to errors and defects,
But not to the error of wanting to understand too much,
Not to the error of wanting to understand only with the
    intelligence,
Not to the defect of requiring the world
To be something other than the world.

24 OCTOBER 1917

Whoever or whatever is at the center of the world
Gave me the outer world as an example of Reality,
And when I say "this is real," even of a feeling,
I can't help but see it in some kind of external space,
In a visual kind of way, outside and apart from me.

Being real means not being inside myself.
My inner self doesn't have any reality I can conceive of.
I know the world exists, but I don't know if I do.
I'm more certain of the existence of my white house
Than of the inner existence of the white house's owner.
I believe in my body more than in my soul,
Because my body's right here in the midst of reality,
It can be seen by others,
It can touch others,
It can sit down and stand up,
Whereas my soul can't be defined except by outer terms.
It exists for me—in the moments when I think it exists—
By borrowing from the World's outer reality.

If the soul is more real
Than the outer world, as you, philosopher, say it is,
Then why was the outer world given to me as reality's
    prototype?
If my feeling is more certain
Than the existence of the thing I feel,
Then why do I feel that thing and why does it appear
Independently of me,

Without needing me to exist—
Me, who am forever bound to myself, forever personal and
    nontransferable?
Why do I move with other people
In a world where we understand each other and coincide,
If the world is what's mistaken and I'm the one who's right?
If the world is a mistake, it's a mistake for everybody,
Whereas each of us is just our own mistake.
Between the two, the world is more in the right.

But why all these questions, unless it's because I'm sick?

On the outer and therefore right days of my life,
On the days when I'm perfectly, naturally lucid,
I feel without feeling that I feel,
I see without knowing that I see,
And the Universe is never so real as then,
The Universe is never (it's not near or far from me
But) so sublimely not-mine.

When in life I say "it's obvious," do I mean "only I can see it"?
When in life I say "it's true," do I mean "that's my opinion"?
When in life I say "it's there," do I mean "it's not there"?
And why should it be any different in philosophy?
We live before we philosophize, we exist before we know
    we do,
And the earlier fact merits at least homage and precedence.
Yes, we are outer before we are inner.
Therefore we are essentially outer.

You say, sick philosopher, every philosopher, that this is
    materialism.
But how can this be materialism, if materialism is a
    philosophy,
If a philosophy, to belong to me, would have to be a
    philosophy of mine,
And none of this is mine, nor am I even I?

24 OCTOBER 1917

War, which inflicts suffering on the world with its
    squadrons,
Is the perfect demonstration of philosophy's error.

War, like everything human, wants to change things.
But nothing wants to change things more than war, and to
    change them so much
And to change them so quickly.

But war causes death.
And death is the universe's disdain for us.
Since it results in death, war proves itself wrong.
Since it's proven wrong, all wanting-to-change-things is
    proven wrong.

Let's leave the outer universe and other people where Nature
    put them.
So much pride and lack of awareness!
So much bustling, having to do things, wanting to leave a
    mark!
When his heart stops beating, the commander of the
    squadrons
Slowly returns to the outer universe.

In Nature's direct chemistry
There's no room for thought.

Humanity is an uprising of slaves.
Humanity is a government usurped by the people,

Existing because usurped, but erring, since to usurp is to
    have no right.

Let the outer world and natural humanity be!
Peace to all prehuman things, including those in man!
Peace to the wholly outer essence of the Universe!

24 OCTOBER 1917

All the opinions ever formed about Nature
Never made a flower bloom or a blade of grass grow.
All the knowledge there is concerning things
Was never something I could seize, like a thing.
If science aspires to be true,
What truer science than that of things without science?
I close my eyes, and the reality of the hard earth I'm lying on
Is so real that even the bones in my back feel it.
Where I have shoulder blades I don't need reason.

29 MAY 1918

O ship setting out on a distant long voyage,
Why don't I miss you the way other people do
After you've vanished from sight?
Because, when I don't see you, you cease to exist.
And if I feel nostalgia for what doesn't exist,
The feeling is in relationship to nothing.
It's not the ship but our own selves that we miss.

29 MAY 1918

Truth, falsehood, certainty, uncertainty . . .
The blind man there on the road also knows these words.
I'm sitting near the top of the steps with my hands folded
On the higher of my crossed knees.
So what are truth, falsehood, certainty and uncertainty?
The blind man stops on the road;
I've taken my hands off my knee.
Do truth, falsehood, certainty and uncertainty remain the
    same?
Something changed in a part of reality—my knees and my
    hands.
What science can explain this?
The blind man continues on his way and my hands keep still.
It's no longer the same time, or the same people, or the same
    anything . . .
To be real is this.

                                                        12 APRIL 1919

Hillside shepherd, so far away from me with your sheep,
Is the happiness you seem to have your happiness or mine?
Does the peace I feel when I see you belong to me or to you?
No, shepherd, neither to you nor to me.
It belongs only to peace and happiness.
You don't have it, because you don't know you have it,
And I don't have it, because I know I do.
It exists on its own, and falls on us like the sun,
Which hits you on the back and warms you up, while you
    indifferently think about something else,
And it hits me in the face and dazzles my eyes, and I think
    only about the sun.

12 APRIL 1919

Between what I see of one field and what I see of another
     field
The figure of a man passes by.
His footsteps move with "him" in the same reality,
But I see him and see them, and they are two separate things.
The "man" moves along with his ideas, in error and a
     foreigner,
While his footsteps move by the ancient system that makes
     legs walk.
I look at him from afar without any opinion.
How perfect in him is the substance he is: his body,
His true reality with no desires or hopes,
Just muscles and the right, impersonal way of using them!

                                        20 APRIL 1919

I'm not in a hurry. In a hurry for what?
The sun and moon aren't in a hurry; they're right.
To hurry is to suppose we can overtake our legs
Or leap over our shadow.
No, I'm not in a hurry.
If I stretch out my arm, I'll reach exactly as far as my arm
    reaches
And not half an inch farther.
I touch where my finger touches, not where I think.
I can only sit down where I am.
This sounds ridiculous, like all absolutely true truths,
But what's really ridiculous is how we're always thinking of
    something else,
And we're always outside it, because we're here.

20 JUNE 1919

Live, you say, in the present.
Live only in the present.

But I don't want the present, I want reality.
I want the things that exist, not the time that measures them.

What is the present?
It's something in relation to the past and the future.
It's something that exists by virtue of other things existing.
I want only reality, the things themselves, without any
    present.

I don't want to include time in my awareness of what exists.
I don't want to think of things as being in the present; I want
    to think of them as things.
I don't want to separate them from themselves, calling them
    present.

I shouldn't even call them real.
I shouldn't call them anything.

I should see them, just see them,
See them until I can no longer think about them,
See them without time or space,
See with no need of anything besides what I'm seeing.
This is the science of seeing, which is no science at all.

19 JULY 1920

You say I'm something more
Than a stone or a plant.
You say: "You feel, you think, and you know
That you think and feel.
Do stones write poems?
Do plants have ideas about the world?"

Yes, there's a difference,
But it's not the difference you suppose,
Because being conscious doesn't oblige me to have theories
    about things;
It only obliges me to be conscious.

If I'm more than a stone or a plant? I don't know.
I'm different. I don't know what more is or what less is.

Is being conscious more than being colorful?
It might be or might not be.
I know only that it's different.
No one can prove that it's more than just different.

I know the stone is real and the plant exists.
I know this because they exist.
I know this because my senses show it to me.
I know I'm real as well.
I know this because my senses show it to me,
Though less clearly than they show me the stone and the
    plant.
That's all I know.

Yes, I write poems, and the stone doesn't write poems.
Yes, I have ideas about the world, and the plant has none.
But stones are not poets, they're stones;
And plants are just plants, not thinkers.
I can say this makes me superior to them
Or I can say it makes me inferior.
But I say no such thing. I say of the stone, "It's a stone."
I say of the plant, "It's a plant."
I say of myself, "It's me."
And I say no more. What more is there to say?

5 JUNE 1922

The first sign of the storm that will strike the day after
    tomorrow,
The first clouds, still white, hanging low in the dull sky . . .
The storm that will strike the day after tomorrow?
I'm certain, but my certainty is a lie.
To be certain is to not be seeing.
The day after tomorrow doesn't exist.
This is what exists:
A blue sky that's a bit hazy and some white clouds on the
    horizon,
With a dark smudge underneath, as if they might turn black.
This is what today is,
And since for the time being today is everything, this is
    everything.
I might be dead—who knows?—the day after tomorrow,
In which case the storm that will strike the day after
    tomorrow
Will be a different storm than it would be if I hadn't died.
I realize that the storm doesn't fall from my eyes,
But if I'm no longer in this world, the world will be
    different—
There will be one person less—
And the storm, falling in a different world, won't be the
    same storm.
In any case, the storm that's going to fall will be the one
    falling when it falls.

10 JULY 1930

RICARDO REIS

*I was born believing in the gods, I was raised in that belief,
and in that belief I will die, loving them. I know what the
pagan feeling is. My only regret is that I can't really explain
how utterly and inscrutably different it is from all other
feelings. Even our calm and the vague stoicism some of us
have bear no resemblance to the calm of antiquity and the
stoicism of the Greeks.*

(FROM RICARDO REIS'S UNFINISHED PREFACE TO HIS *ODES*)

I love the roses of Adonis's gardens.
Yes, Lydia, I love those wingèd roses,
        Which one day are born
        And on that day die.
Light for them is eternal, since
They are born after sunrise and end
        Before Apollo quits
        His visible journey.
Let us also make our lives *one day*,
Consciously forgetting there's night, Lydia,
        Before and after
        The little we endure.

11 JULY 1914

To Alberto Caeiro

Peaceful, Master,
Are all the hours
We lose if we place,
As in a vase,
Flowers on our
Losing them.

There are in our life
No sorrows or joys.
So let us learn,
Wisely unworried,
Not how to live life
But to let it go by,

Keeping forever
Peaceful and calm,
Taking children
For our teachers
And letting Nature
Fill our eyes . . .

Along the river
Or along the road,
Wherever we are,
Always remaining
In the same, easy
Repose of living . . .

Time passes
And tells us nothing.
We grow old.
Let us know how,
With a certain mischief,
To feel ourselves pass.

Taking action
Serves no purpose.
No one can resist
The atrocious god
Who always devours
His own children.

Let us pick flowers.
Let us lightly
Wet our hands
In the calm rivers,
So as to learn
To be calm like them.

Sunflowers forever
Beholding the sun,
We will serenely
Depart from life,
Without even the regret
Of having lived.

12 JUNE 1914

The god Pan isn't dead.
In each field that shows
Ceres' naked breasts
To the smiles of Apollo,
Sooner or later
You will see the god Pan,
Immortal, appear.

The Christians' sad god
Killed none of the others.
Christ is one more god,
One that was perhaps missing.

Pan still offers
The piping of his flute
To the ears of Ceres
Reclining in the fields.

The gods are the same,
Always clear and calm,
Full of eternity
And disdain for us,
Bringing day and night
And golden harvests
Not in order to give us
Day and night and wheat
But for some other, divine
And incidental purpose.

12 JUNE 1914

Snow covers the sunlit hills in the distance,
But the calm cold that smoothes and whets
          The darts of the high sun
          Has already turned mild.
Today, Neaera, let us not hide:
Since we are nothing, we lack nothing.
          We have nothing to expect
          And feel cold in the sun.
But such as it is, let us enjoy
This moment, somewhat solemn in our joy,
          While waiting for death
          As for something we know.

16 JUNE 1914

The day's paleness is tinged with gold.
The curves of parched trunks and branches gleam
          Like dew in the winter sun.
          The chill air shivers.
Exiled from the ancient land of my beliefs,
Consoled only by calling to mind the gods,
          I warm my trembling body
          With a different sun from this:
The sun of the Parthenon and Acropolis
Which lit up the slow and weighty steps
          Of Aristotle speaking.
          But Epicurus speaks more
To my heart with his tender, earthly voice;
His attitude toward the gods is itself divine,
          Serene and seeing life
          At the distance where it lies.

19 JUNE 1914

Wise the man who enjoys the world's spectacle
        And drinks without recalling
        That he has drunk before,
        For whom everything is new
        And will never wither.
Crown him with ivy, vines, and twined roses.
        He knows that life
        Is just passing by
        And that Atropos's shears
        Cut the flower and cut him.
He knows how to hide this with the color of the wine
        And to erase, with its orgiastic
        Flavor, the taste of time,
        As the frenzy of the bacchantes
        Quells a weeping voice.
And he waits, a calm drinker and almost happy,
        Only desiring
        With a desire scarcely felt
        That the abominable wave
        Not wet him too soon.

19 JUNE 1914

Each thing, in its time, has its time.
The trees do not blossom in winter,
         Nor does the white cold
         Cover the fields in spring.
The heat that the day required of us
Belongs not to the night that's falling, Lydia.
         Let's love with greater calm
         Our uncertain life.
Sitting by the fire, weary not from our work
But because it's the hour for weariness,
         Let's not force our voice
         To be more than a secret.
And may our words of reminiscence
(Stirred up by the dark departure of the sun)
         Be spoken at intervals,
         Haphazardly.
Let's remember the past by degrees,
And may the stories told back then,
         Now twice-told stories,
         Speak to us
Of the flowers that in our distant childhood
We picked with another kind of pleasure
         And another consciousness
         As we gazed at the world.
And so, Lydia, sitting there by the fire
As if there forever, like household gods,
         Let's mend the past
         As if mending clothes

In the disquiet that resting brings to our lives
When all we do is think of what
            We were, and outside
            There's just night.

                                        30 JULY 1914

Bearing in mind our likeness with the gods
        Let us, for our own good,
See ourselves as exiled deities
        In possession of life
By virtue of an ancient authority
        Going back to Jove.

Proud masters over our own selves,
        Let's use existence
Like a villa the gods have given us
        To forget the hot summer.

It's not worth our while to use in another,
        More fretful manner
Our uncertain existence, a doomed stream
        Of the somber river.

Like the calm, implacable Fate
        That reigns above the gods,
Let's construct a voluntary fate
        Above ourselves,
So that when it oppresses us, it is we
        Who'll be our oppressors.
And when we enter into night, we'll enter
        By our own two feet.

                                30 JULY 1914

The only freedom the gods grant
    Is this: to submit
Of our own free will to their rule.
    We should do just that,
Since only in the illusion of freedom
    Does freedom exist.

It is what the gods, subject
    To eternal fate, do
To maintain their calm and steady,
    Ancient conviction
That their life is divine and free.
    Imitating the gods,

No freer on Olympus than we are,
    Let's build our lives
Like those who build castles of sand
    To delight the eyes,
And the gods will know how to thank us
    For being so like them.

30 JULY 1914

Remember, with quick steps, on the white beach
Darkened by the foam, the ancient rhythm
        That bare feet know,
        That rhythm repeated
By nymphs when they tap the song of the dance
In the shade of the trees; you, children
        Not yet concerned
        With concerns, revive
That noisy circle while Apollo bends,
Like a high branch, the blue curve he gilds,
        And the tide, high or low,
        Flows without ceasing.

                        9 AUGUST 1914

We've always had the confident vision
That other beings, angels or gods,
        Reign above us
        And move us to act.
Just as in the fields our actions
On the cattle, which they don't understand,
        Coerce and compel them
        Without their knowing why,
So too our human will and mind
Are the hands by which others lead us
        To wherever they want us
        To desire to go.

16 OCTOBER 1914

Lost from the way, you clutch your sterile,
Toilsome days in bundles of hard wood
     And think you are living
     Life without illusions.
Your wood is only weight you carry
To where you'll have no fire to warm you,
     Nor will the shades we become
     Endure weight on their shoulders.
To rest up you don't rest. If you pass
Something on, pass not wealth but the example
     Of how a brief life is enough,
     Brief and not too hard.
We use little of the little we scarcely have.
Work tires, and the gold isn't ours.
     Our own fame laughs at us,
     For we won't see it
When, brought down by the Fates, suddenly
We'll be ancient, solemn figures,
     Ever more shadowy,
     Until the fatal meeting—
The dark boat on the gloomy river,
And the nine embraces of Stygian cold,
     And the insatiable lap
     Of the land of Pluto.

[LATE 1914 OR 1915]

THE CHESS PLAYERS

I've heard that during some war or other
        Fought by Persia,
As invaders rampaged through the City
        And the women screamed,
Two chess players kept on playing
        Their endless game.

In the shade of a leafy tree they stared
        At the old chessboard,
And next to each player was a mug of wine,
        Solemnly ready
To quench his thirst in the moments when,
        Having made his move,
He could sit back and relax, waiting
        On his opponent.

Houses were burning, walls were torn down
        And coffers plundered;
Women were raped and propped against
        The crumbling walls;
Children, pierced by spears, were so much
        Blood in the streets . . .
But the chess players stayed where they were,
        Close to the city
And far from its clamor, and kept on playing
        Their game of chess.

Even if, in the bleak wind's messages,
        They heard the screams
And, upon reflection, knew in their hearts
        That surely their women
And their tender daughters were being raped
        In the nearby distance,
Even if, in the moment they thought this,
        A fleeting shadow
Passed over their hazy, oblivious brows,
        Soon their calm eyes
Returned with confident attention
        To the old chessboard.

When the ivory king's in danger, who cares
        About the flesh and blood
Of sisters and mothers and children?
        When the rook can't cover
The retreat of the white queen, what
        Does pillaging matter?
And when with sure hand the opponent's king
        Is placed in check,
Sons and daughters dying in the distance
        Weigh little on one's soul.

Even if the infuriated face
        Of an invading warrior
Should suddenly peer over the wall and cause
        The solemn chess player
To fall right there in a bloody heap,
        The moment before that
Was still devoted to the favorite game
        Of the supremely indifferent.

Let cities fall and people suffer,
        Let life and freedom
Perish, let secure, ancestral properties
        Be burned and uprooted,
But when war interrupts the game, make sure

The king's not in check
And the most advanced white pawn is ready
        To redeem the rook.

My brothers in loving Epicurus
        And in understanding him
According to our view rather than his,
        Let this story
Of the calm chess players teach us how
        To spend our lives.

Let serious things scarcely matter to us
        And grave things weigh little,
And let our natural impulses yield
        To the futile pleasure
(In the peaceful shade of the trees)
        Of playing a good game.

Whatever we take from this useless life,
        Be it glory or fame,
Love, science, or life itself,
        Let's think of it only
As the memory of a well-played game
        And a match won
        Against a better player.

Glory weighs like an overlarge burden
        And fame like a fever,
Love wearies, for it ardently searches,
        Science never finds,
And life grieves, for it knows it is passing . . .
        The game of chess
Absorbs us completely but causes no grief
        When lost, for it's nothing.

Ah, in the shade that unconsciously loves us
        And with a mug of wine
At our side, intent only on the useless

Effort of the chess game,
Even if the game is only a dream
And we have no partner,
Let's do as the Persians of this story:
Wherever out there,
Near or faraway, war and our country
And life are calling us,
Let them call in vain, while we sit
In the friendly shade,
Dreaming up partners, and the game goes on
In dreamy indifference.

1 JUNE 1916

Not you, Christ, do I hate or reject.
In you as in the other, older gods I believe.
        But for me you are not more
        Or less than they, just younger.
I do hate and calmly abhor those who want
To place you above the other gods, your equals.
        I want you where you are, not higher
        Nor lower than them—just yourself.
A sad god, needed perhaps since there was none
Like you, you're new to the Pantheon
        And our faith—not higher nor purer
        But different from the gods of other things.
Take care, obsessive idolater of Christ, for life
Is multiple, all days differ from all others,
        And only if we're multiple like them
        Will we be true to ourselves and alone.

9 OCTOBER 1916

I suffer, Lydia, from the fear of destiny.
Any tiny thing that might
Give rise to a new order in my life
        Frightens me, Lydia.
Anything whatsoever that changes
The smooth course of my existence,
Though it change it for something better,
        Because it means change,
I hate and don't want it. May the gods
Allow my life to be a continuous,
Perfectly flat plain, running
        To where it ends.
Though I never taste glory and never
Receive love or due respect from others,
It will suffice that life is just life
        And that I live it.

26 MAY 1917

A verse repeating
A cool breeze,
Summer in the fields,
And the deserted courtyard
Languishing in the sunlight . . .

Or, in winter, the snowy
Summits in the distance,
The fireside where we sit
Singing handed-down tales,
And a poem to tell all this . . .

The gods grant us
Few pleasures beyond
These, which are nothing.
But they also grant
That we want no others.

29 JANUARY 1921

Securely I sit on the steadfast column
          Of the verses in which I'll remain,
Not fearing the endless future influx
          Of eras and of oblivion,
For when the mind intently observes
          In itself the world's reflections,
It becomes their plasma, and the world is what
          Makes art, not the mind. Thus
On the plaque the outer moment engraves
          Its being, and there endures.

[JANUARY 1921]

You'll become only who you always were.
What the gods give they give at the start.
        Fate assigns you your fate
        Just once, for you're but one.
Little is attained by the effort you exert
In accord with your native ability.
        Little, if you were not
        Conceived for more.
Be glad to be who you can't avoid being.
You will still have the vast sky
        Above and the green or dry
        Earth, depending on the season.

12 MAY 1921

Everyone fulfills the destiny they must fulfill
And desires the destiny they desire;
      They don't fulfill what they desire
      Nor desire what they fulfill.
Like stones that border flower beds
We are arranged by Fate, and there remain,
      Our lot having placed us
      Where we had to be placed.
Let's have no better knowledge of what
Was our due than that it was our due.
      Let's fulfill what we are.
      Nothing more are we given.

                       29 JULY 1923

I don't sing of night, since in my song
The sun I sing of will end in night.
         I know what I'm forgetting.
         I sing to forget it.
Could I only stop, even if in a dream,
The course of Apollo and know myself,
         Even if mad, as the twin
         Of an imperishable hour!

2 SEPTEMBER 1923

I don't want your presents,
In which you cannot help
But deny me what you're giving.
You give me what I'll lose,
Weeping its loss twice over,
As something of you and of me.

Promise to give it, without giving
Me anything, since then the loss
Will occur in my hopes
More than in my memory.

I'll only regret that life
Goes on, seeing the days pass
While what it hopes for still
Doesn't come, and it's nothing.

2 SEPTEMBER 1923

I want the flower you are, not the one you give.
Why refuse me what I'm not asking you for?
    You'll have time to refuse
    After you've given.
Flower, be my flower! If in this unyielding state
The dire sphinx's paw should pluck you, you'll roam
    Forever, an absurd shadow,
    Seeking what you didn't give.

21 OCTOBER 1923

*Ad Caeiri manes magistri**

The new summer that newly brings
Apparently new flowers renews
      The ancient green
      Of the revived leaves.
No more will the barren abyss, which silently
Swallows what we hardly are, give back
      To the clear light of day
      His living presence.
No more; and the progeny to whom his thought
Gave the life of reason, pleads for him in vain,
      For the Styx's nine keys
      Lock but do not open.
He who was like a god among singers,
Who heard the voices that called from Olympus
      And, hearing, listened
      And understood, is now nothing.
But weave for him still the garlands you weave.
Whom will you crown if you don't crown him?
      Present them as funerary
      Offerings with no cult.
But let not the loam or Hades touch
His fame; and you, whom Ulysses founded,
      You, with your seven hills,
      Take maternal pride,

---

* "To the Manes of master Caeiro." The penultimate stanza refers to Lisbon, which has seven hills and was founded, according to legend, by Ulysses. Caeiro, according to his "biography," was born in Lisbon.

Equal, since him, to the seven cities
Claiming Homer, to alcaic Lesbos
    And to seven-gated Thebes,
    Ogygian mother of Pindar.

22 OCTOBER 1923

How short a time is the longest life
And our youth in it! Ah Chloe, Chloe,
    If I don't love, don't drink
    And don't naturally shun thinking,
The implacable law oppresses me,
Time's endless, imposed hours afflict me,
    And to my ears comes
    The sound of the rushes
On the hidden shore where cold lilies
Grow in stygian soil and the current,
    A groaning murmur,
    Knows not where the day is.

24 OCTOBER 1923

Plowing his scant field or solemnly
Beholding it as if he were beholding
A son, this man enjoys, uncertainly,
       The unthinking life.
Changes occurring in the false borders
Do not thwart his plow, nor is he
Troubled by whatever councils govern
       The fate of patient peoples.
Little more in the present of the future
Than the grass he pulled up, he lives securely
His old life that won't return but endures,
       Sons, different and his own.

16 NOVEMBER 1923

Don't try to build in the space you suppose
Is future, Lydia, and don't promise yourself
Tomorrow. Quit waiting and be who you are
          Today. You alone are your life.
Don't plot your destiny, for you are not future.
Between the cup you empty and the same cup
Refilled, who knows whether your fortune
          Won't interpose the abyss?

[1923?]

Hour by hour the ancient face of repeated
Beings changes, and hour by hour,
         Thinking, we get older.
Everything passes, unknown, and the knower
Who remains knows he's ignorant. But nothing,
         Aware or unaware, returns.
Equals, therefore, of what's not our equal,
Let us preserve, in the heat we remember,
         The flame of the spent hour.

16 NOVEMBER 1923

Already over my vain brow
The hair of that youth who died is graying.
          My eyes shine less today.
My lips have lost their right to kisses.
If you still love me, for love's sake stop loving:
          Don't cheat on me with me.

                         13 JUNE 1926

The leaf won't return to the branch it left,
Nor from its dust will a new leaf be formed.
The moment, which ends as this one begins,
        Has died forever.
The vain, uncertain future promises
No more than this repeated experience
Of the mortal lot and forlorn condition
        Of things and of myself.
And so, in this universal river
Where I'm not a wave, but waves,
I languidly flow, with no requests
        And no gods to hear them.

28 SEPTEMBER 1926

Fruits are given by trees that live,
Not by the wishful mind, which adorns
        Itself with ashen flowers
        From the abyss within.
How many kingdoms in minds and in things
Your imagination has carved! That many
        You've lost, pre-dethroned,
        Without ever having them.
Against great opposition you'll conquer
Nothing uniquely yours. Life is invincible.
        Abdicate and be
        King of yourself.

6 DECEMBER 1926

Dreamed pleasure is pleasure, albeit in a dream.
What we suppose of ourselves we become,
        If with a focused mind
        We persist in believing it.
So do not censure my way of thinking
About things, beings, and fate.
        For myself I create as much
        As I create for myself.
Outside me, indifferent to what I think,
Fate is fulfilled. But I fulfill myself
        Within the small ambit
        Of what's given to me to be mine.

30 JANUARY 1927

To nothing can your hands, now things, appeal,
Nor can your now stiff lips persuade,
    In the oppressive depths
    Of damp, inflicted earth.
Perhaps just the smile from when you loved
Embalms you, far away, and in our memories
    Lifts you to what you were,
    Today a rotten hive.
And the useless name that your dead body
Used, like a soul, when alive on earth
    Is forgotten. This ode engraves
    An anonymous smile.

MAY 1927

How many enjoy the enjoyment of enjoying
Without enjoying their enjoyment, and divide it
          Between themselves and others
          Noticing their enjoyment.
Lydia, forego the trappings of enjoyment,
For we have but one enjoyment; we cannot
          Give it to others as a prize
          For noticing that we enjoy.
We have but one self, so let's enjoy others
By enjoying them for our own sake, not theirs.
          Learn what your body,
          Your boundary, teaches you.

9 OCTOBER 1927

Sleep is good because we wake up from it
And know that it's good. If death is sleep,
        We'll wake up from it;
        If it isn't, and we won't,
Then let's reject it with all that we are
For as long as the undecided jailer
        Allows our condemned
        Bodies to continue.
Lydia, I prefer the vilest life
To death, which I don't know, and for you
        I pick flowers, votive
        Offerings of a lowly destiny.

19 NOVEMBER 1927

The fleeting track made by the vanished foot
In the soft grass, the echo that hollowly rolls,
> The shadow that grows blacker,
> The whiteness a ship leaves in its wake—
So too the soul, no greater or better, quits souls;
What's passed leaves what's passing. Memory forgets.
> Once dead, we keep dying.
> Lydia, we exist for ourselves.

25 JANUARY 1928

Whatever ceases is death, and the death
Is ours if it ceases for us. A bush
      Withers, and with it
      Goes part of my life.
In all I've observed, part of me remained.
Whatever I've seen, when it passed I passed,
      Memory not distinguishing
      What I've seen from what I've been.

7 JUNE 1928

Let my fate deny me everything except
       To see it, for I, an unstrict
Stoic, want to relish every letter
       Of the sentence engraved by Destiny.

21 NOVEMBER 1928

When, Lydia, our autumn arrives
With the winter it harbors, let's reserve
A thought, not for the future spring,
          Which belongs to others,
Nor for the summer, to which we've died,
But for what remains of what is passing:
The present yellow that the leaves live
          And that makes them different.

13 JUNE 1930

Hesitant, as if forgotten by Aeolus,
The morning breeze caresses the field,
        And the sun begins to glimmer.
Let us, Lydia, not wish in this hour
For more sun than this or for a stronger breeze
        Than the one that's small and exists.

13 JUNE 1930

Weak in vice, weak in virtue,
Not even in fury does weak humanity
        Know more than the norm.
Equals, but different, we govern ourselves
By our own norm, which, though harsh,
        Will be freedom.
To be free is to be your own imposed norm,
Like others except in the broad and harsh
        Control and use of yourself.

9 JULY 1930

Not just those who envy and hate us
Limit and oppress us; those who love us
     Limit us no less.
May the Gods grant me, stripped of all
Affections, the cold freedom of the heights
     Of nothingness. Wanting little,
A man has everything. Wanting nothing,
He's free. Not having and not desiring,
     He's equal, though man, to the Gods.

1 NOVEMBER 1930

Rule or keep quiet. Don't squander yourself,
    Giving what you don't have.
What good is the Caesar you might have been?
    Enjoy being the little you are.
The hovel you're given is a better shelter
    Than the palace you're owed.

27 SEPTEMBER 1931

If each thing has its corresponding god,
Why shouldn't I have a god as well?
            Why shouldn't it be me?
It's in me that this god moves, for I feel.
I clearly see the outside world—
            Things, people, with no soul.

DECEMBER 1931

No one loves anyone else; he loves
What he finds of himself in the other.
Don't fret if others don't love you. They feel
        Who you are, and you're a stranger.
Be who you are, even if never loved.
Secure in yourself, you'll suffer
        Few sorrows.

                                        10 AUGUST 1932

Nothing of nothing remains. We're nothing.
In the sun and air we put off briefly
The unbreathable darkness of damp earth
          Whose weight we'll have to bear—
Postponed corpses that procreate.

Laws passed, statues admired, odes finished—
All have their grave. If we, heaps of flesh
Made sanguine by an inner sun,
          Must finally set, why not they?
We're tales telling tales, nothing . . .

                              28 SEPTEMBER 1932

To be great, be whole: don't exaggerate
    Or leave out any part of you.
Be complete in each thing. Put all you are
    Into the least of your acts.
So too in each lake, with its lofty life,
    The whole moon shines.

14 FEBRUARY 1933

Calm because I'm unknown,
And myself because I'm calm,
I want to fill my days
With wanting nothing else.

For those whom wealth touches,
Gold irritates the skin.
For those on whom fame smiles,
Life turns dreary.

On those who shine with the sun
Of happiness, night will fall.
But those who hope for nothing
Are glad for whatever comes.

2 MARCH 1933

Each day you didn't enjoy wasn't yours:
You just got through it. Whatever you live
      Without enjoying, you don't live.
You don't have to love or drink or smile.
The sun's reflection in a puddle of water
      Is enough, if it pleases you.
Happy those who, placing their delight
In slight things, are never deprived
      Of each day's natural blessings!

14 MARCH 1933

Since we do nothing in this confused world
That lasts or that, lasting, is worth anything,
And even what's useful for us we lose
        All too soon, with our own lives,
Let us prefer the pleasure of the moment
To an absurd concern with the future,
Whose only certainty is our present harm
        That pays for its prosperity.
Tomorrow doesn't exist. This moment
Alone is mine, and I'm just who
Exists in this instant, which might be the last
        Of the self I pretend to be.

                        16 MARCH 1933

You're alone. No one knows it. Hush and feign.
        But feign without feigning.
Hope for nothing that's not already in you.
        Each man in himself is everything.
You have sun if there's sun, trees if you seek them,
        Fortune if fortune is yours.

6 APRIL 1933

I love what I see because one day
            I'll stop seeing it. I also
            Love it because it is.
In this calm moment when I feel myself
            By loving more than by being,
            I love all existence and myself.
No better thing could the primitive gods
            Give me, were they to return—
            They, who also know nothing.

11 OCTOBER 1934

All I ask the gods to grant me is that
I ask them for nothing. Good luck is a yoke
      And to be happy oppresses,
      For it's an emotional state.
I want to raise my not easy nor uneasy,
Purely calm being above the plane
      Where people rejoice or grieve.

My hand that destroys
The heap of ants
Must seem to them of divine origin,
But I don't consider myself divine.
Likewise the gods
Perhaps do not see
Themselves as gods, being gods in our eyes
Only because they're greater than us.
Whatever the case,
Let's not commit
Completely to a faith, perhaps unfounded,
In those we believe to be gods.

The false season changed four times
In the false year of the changeless course
        Of time's progression.
Dryness follows greenness, and greenness dryness,
And no one knows which is first, which
        Is last, and they end.

Of the gods I ask only to be ignored.
Without good or bad luck, I'll be free,
        Like the wind that's the life
        Of the air, which is nothing.
Hatred and love both seek us out;
Both oppress us, each in its own way.
        Those to whom the gods
        Grant nothing are free.

ÁLVARO DE CAMPOS

I don't believe in anything but the existence of my sensations; I have no other certainty, not even of the outer universe conveyed to me by those sensations. I don't see the outer universe, I don't hear the outer universe, I don't touch the outer universe. I see my visual impressions; I hear my auditory impressions; I touch my tactile impressions. It's not with the eyes but with the soul that I see; it's not with the ears but with the soul that I hear; it's not with the skin but with the soul that I touch. And if someone should ask me what the soul is, I'll answer that it's me.

(FROM ÁLVARO DE CAMPOS'S *NOTES FOR THE MEMORY OF MY MASTER CAEIRO*)

OPIARY

It's before I take opium that my soul is sick.
To feel life is to wilt like a convalescent,
And so I seek in the solace of opium
An East to the east of the East.

This life on board will surely kill me.
Fever rages in me day and night.
And although I wear myself out searching,
I can't find the spring to set me right.

In paradox and astral incompetence,
I live a life of golden days,
A wave in which dignity's a descent
And pleasures are ganglia of my malaise.

It's through a clockwork of disasters,
A mechanism of pseudo-flywheels,
That I walk among visions of gallows
In a garden of stemless, floating flowers.

I stagger through the handiwork
Of an inner life of lace and lacquer,
Convinced I have at home the knife
That beheaded John the Baptist.

I'm atoning for a crime in a suitcase
That my grandfather committed for fun.
My nerves hang from the gibbet by the dozen,
And I've fallen into the pit of opium.

With the soporific nudge of morphine
I lose myself in throbbing transparencies:
On a diamond-studded night the moon
Rises as if it were my Destiny.

Always a terrible student, now
I do nothing but watch the ship sail on
Through the Suez Canal, taking with it
My life, mere camphor in the dawn.

Gone are the days I put to good use.
All I earned from my work was fatigue,
Which is today like an arm around my neck
That chokes me and keeps me from falling.

I was a child like everyone else.
Born in a small town, Portuguese,
I've met people from England
Who say I speak English perfectly.

I'd like to have poems and stories
Published by Plon and in *Mércure*,
But I doubt this life—a voyage
Without storms—can long endure!

Although it has its amusing moments,
Life on board is a dreary affair.
I talk with Germans, Swedes and Brits,
But the pain of living is always there.

To sail east to see China and India
Wasn't worth it after all.
There's only one way of living,
And the earth's the same, and small.

Opium for me is a medicine.
I'm convalescing from the Moment.
I live on thought's ground floor,
And to see Life go by is a torment.

I smoke. I yawn. Were there only an earth
Where far to the east didn't become west!
Why did I visit the India that exists,
When the only India is the soul I possess?

Disgrace was my only inheritance.
The gypsies made off with my Fortune.
Perhaps not even near death will I find
A shelter to make my cold self warm.

I pretended to study engineering.
Lived in Scotland. Saw Ireland on holiday.
My heart mills around the doors of Happiness,
Begging for alms like a little old lady.

Don't call, iron ship, at Port Said!
Turn right, I don't even know where to.
I kill time with the count in the smoking room—
A swindling French count who lingers at funerals.

I glumly return to Europe, destined
To become a sleepwalking poet.
I'm a monarchist but not a Catholic,
And I'd like to be someone of note.

I'd like to have money and beliefs,
To be various dull people I've seen.
As things stand now, I'm nothing
But a passenger on a ship at sea.

I don't have any personality.
Even the cabin boy makes a more lasting
Impression with his lofty bearing
Of a Scottish laird who's been fasting.

I don't belong anywhere. My country
Is wherever I'm not. I'm sick and weak.
The steward is a rogue. He saw me
With the Swedish lady . . . and winked.

One day I'll cause a scandal on board
Just to make the others tattle.
Fed up with life, I think it's natural
That sometimes I fly off the handle.

I spend all day smoking and drinking
American drugs that numb every pain—
I, who am already naturally drunk!
My rose-like nerves need a better brain.

How strange that I can't even feel
The talent I have for writing these verses!
Life is a big house in the country
That bores any sensitive person.

The English were made for existence.
No other people has a closer alliance
With Tranquility. Insert a coin
And out comes an Englishman, all smiles.

I belong to that class of Portuguese
Who, once India was discovered, were out
Of work. Death is a sure thing.
This is something I often think about.

To hell with life and having to live it!
I don't even read the book by my bed.
I'm sick of the East. It's a painted mat
Whose beauty, once rolled up, is dead.

So I fall into opium. It's too much
To expect me to live one of those ideal
Lives. Honest people with set times
For going to bed and eating meals

Can go to the devil! Yes, this is envy.
These keyed-up nerves are my demise.

If only some ship could take me to where
I'd want only what I see with my eyes.

Who am I fooling? I'd still get bored.
I'd want a yet stronger opium, by which
To have dreams that would finish me off
And pitch me into a muddy ditch.

Fever! If what I have isn't fever,
Then I don't know what fever is.
The essential fact is that I'm sick.
This hare, friends, has lost its vim.

Night has fallen. The bugle has sounded
The first call to dinner: time to get spruce.
Social life beckons! We'll promenade
Like dogs till we work our collars loose.

This story is bound to turn out
Badly, with blood and a gun
(Hooray!) at the end of my disquiet,
For which nothing can be done.

Whoever bothers to look at me
Must find me banal . . . A young chap, right!
Even my monocle makes me belong
To a universal stereotype.

How many like me sail on ocean liners
And, like me, are mystics!
How many, under their de rigueur jackets,
Feel, like me, the horror of existence!

If at least I could be as interesting
On the outside as I am inwardly!
I'm spiraling toward the Maelstrom's center.
My doing nothing is what condemned me.

A do-nothing, yes, but with good reason!
I wish I could hold everyone in disdain
And, even if dressed in a shabby suit,
Be a hero, handsome, damned, or insane!

I feel like sticking my hands in my mouth
And biting until I wince with pain.
It would be an original activity
And amuse the others, the so-called sane.

Absurdity, like a flower from the India
I never found in India, sprouts
In my sick and tired brain. May God
Change my life or else snuff it out . . .

Let me stay here, in this chair,
Until they pack me into a casket.
I was born to be a mandarin
But lack the serenity, tea, and mat.

I'd love to fall from where I am now
Through a trapdoor—clack!—into my grave!
Life tastes to me like mild tobacco.
I never did more than smoke life away.

What I want finally is faith and peace
And to get these sensations under control.
Put an end to this, God! Open the sluices!
Enough of this comedy in my soul!

MARCH 1914.
ABOARD SHIP IN THE SUEZ CANAL.

TRIUMPHAL ODE

By the painful light of the factory's huge electric lamps
I write in a fever.
I write gnashing my teeth, rabid for the beauty of all this,
For this beauty completely unknown to the ancients.

O wheels, O gears, eternal *r-r-r-r-r-r-r*!
Bridled convulsiveness of raging mechanisms!
Raging in me and outside me,
Through all my dissected nerves,
Through all the feelers of my every sensory organ!
My lips are parched, O great modern noises,
From hearing you at too close a range,
And my head burns with the desire to proclaim you
In an explosive song telling my every sensation,
An explosiveness contemporaneous with you, O machines!

Gaping deliriously at the engines as at a tropical landscape
—Great human tropics of iron and fire and energy—
I sing, I sing the present, and the past and future too,
Because the present is all the past and all the future:
Plato and Virgil exist in the machines and electric lights
For the simple reason that Virgil and Plato once existed and
were human,
And bits of an Alexander the Great from perhaps the fiftieth
century
As well as atoms that will seethe in the brain of a
hundredth-century Aeschylus

Go round these transmission belts and pistons and flywheels,
Roaring, grinding, thumping, humming, rattling,
Caressing my body all over with one caress of my soul.

If I could express my whole being like an engine!
If I could be complete like a machine!
If I could go triumphantly through life like the latest model
    car!
If at least I could inject all this into my physical being,
Rip myself wide open, and become pervious
To all the perfumes from the oils and hot coals
Of this stupendous, artificial and insatiable black flora!

Brotherhood with all dynamics!
Promiscuous fury of being a moving part
In the cosmopolitan iron rumble
Of unflagging trains,
In the freight-carrying toil of ships,
In the slow and smooth turning of cranes,
In the disciplined tumult of factories,
And in the humming, monotonic near-silence of transmission
    belts!

Productive European hours, wedged
Between machines and practical tasks!
Big cities pausing for a moment in cafés,
In cafés, those oases of useless chatter
Where the sounds and gestures of the Useful
Crystallize and precipitate,
And with them the wheels, cogwheels and ball bearings of
    Progress!
New soulless Minerva of wharfs and train stations!
New enthusiasms commensurate with the Moment!
Iron keels smiling on docksides,
Or raised out of the water, on harbor slipways!
International, transatlantic, Canadian Pacific activity!
Lights and feverishly wasted hours in bars, in hotels,
At Longchamps, at Derbies and at Ascots,

And Piccadillies and Avenues de l'Opéra entering straight
Into my soul!

Hey streets, hey squares, hey bustling crowd!
Everything that passes or that stops before shop windows!
Businessmen, bums, con men in dressy clothes,
Proud members of aristocratic clubs,
Squalid, dubious characters, and vaguely happy family men
Who are paternal even in the gold chains crossing their vests
From one to another pocket!
Everything that passes, passing without ever passing!
The overemphatic presence of prostitutes;
The interesting banality (and who knows what's inside?)
Of bourgeois ladies, usually mother and daughter,
Walking down the street on some errand or other;
The falsely feminine grace of sauntering homosexuals;
And all the simply elegant people who parade down the
    street
And who also, after all, have a soul!

(Ah, how I'd love to be the pimp of all this!)

The dazzling beauty of graft and corruption,
Delicious financial and diplomatic scandals,
Politically motivated assaults on the streets,
And every now and then the comet of a regicide
Lighting up with Awe and Fanfare the usual
Clear skies of everyday Civilization!

Fraudulent reports in the newspapers,
Insincerely sincere political articles,
Checkout counter news, crime stories—
Two columns and continued on the next page!
The fresh smell of printer's ink!
The posters that were just put up, still wet!
Yellow books in white wrappers—*vient de paraître*!
How I love all of you, every last one of you!
How I love all of you, in every way possible,

With my eyes, ears, and sense of smell,
With touch (how much it means for me to touch you!)
And with my mind, like an antenna that quivers because of you!
Ah, how all my senses lust for you!

Fertilizers, steam threshers, breakthroughs in farming!
Agricultural chemistry, and commerce a quasi-science!
O sample cases of traveling salesmen,
Those traveling salesmen who are Industry's knights-errant,
Human extensions of the factories and quiet offices!

O fabrics in shop windows! O mannequins! O latest fashions!
O useless items that everyone wants to buy!
Hello enormous department stores!
Hello electric signs that flash on, glare, and disappear!
Hello everything used to build today, to make it different
     from yesterday!
Hey cement, reinforced concrete, new technologies!
The improvements in gloriously lethal weapons!
Armor, cannons, machine-guns, submarines, airplanes!

I love all of you and all things like a beast.
I love you carnivorously,
Pervertedly, wrapping my eyes
All around you, O great and banal, useful and useless things,
O absolutely modern things my contemporaries,
O present and proximate form
Of the immediate system of the Universe!
New metallic and dynamic Revelation of God!

O factories, O laboratories, O music halls, O amusement
     parks,
O battleships, O bridges, O floating docks—
In my restless, ardent mind
I possess you like a beautiful woman,
I completely possess you like a beautiful woman who isn't
     loved
But who fascinates the man who happens to meet her.

Hey-ya façades of big stores!
Hey-ya elevators of tall buildings!
Hey-ya major cabinet reshufflings!
Policy decisions, parliaments, budget officers,
Trumped-up budgets!
(A budget is as natural as a tree
And a parliament as beautiful as a butterfly.)

Hi-ya the fascination of everything in life,
Because everything is life, from the diamonds in shop windows
To the mysterious bridge of night between the stars
And the ancient, solemn sea that laps the shores
And is mercifully the same
As when Plato was really Plato
In his real presence, in his flesh that had a soul,
And he talked with Aristotle, who was not to be his disciple.

I could be shredded to death by an engine
And feel a woman's sweet surrender when possessed.
Toss me into the furnaces!
Throw me under passing trains!
Thrash me aboard ships!
Masochism through machines!
Some modern sort of sadism, and me, and the hubbub!

Alley-oop jockey who won the Derby,
Oh to sink my teeth into your two-colored cap!

(To be so tall that I couldn't pass through any door!
Ah, gazing is for me a sexual perversion!)

Hi-ya, hi-ya, hi-ya, cathedrals!
Let me bash my head against the edges of your stones,
And be picked up from the ground, a bloody mess,
Without anyone knowing who I am!

O streetcars, cable cars, subways,
Graze and scrape me until I rave in ecstasy!

Hey-ya, hey-ya, hey-ya-ho!
Laugh in my face,
O cars full of carousers and whores,
O daily swarm of pedestrians neither sad nor happy,
Motley anonymous river where I'd love to swim but can't!
Ah, what complex lives, what things inside their homes!
Ah, to know all about them, their financial troubles,
Their domestic quarrels, their unsuspected depravities,
Their thoughts when all alone in their bedrooms,
And their gestures when no one can see them!
Not to know these things is to know nothing at all,
     O rage,
O rage that like a fever or a hunger or a mad lust
Makes my face contract and my hands shake
With weird twitches in the middle of the crowds
Pushing and shoving on the streets!

Ah, and the ordinary, sordid people who always look the same,
Who use swearwords like regular words,
Whose sons steal from grocers
And whose eight-year-old daughters (and I think this is
     sublime!)
Masturbate respectable-looking men in stairwells.
The rabble who spend all day on scaffolds and walk home
On narrow lanes of almost unreal squalor.
Wondrous human creatures who live like dogs,
Who are beneath all moral systems,
For whom no religion was invented,
No art created,
No politics formulated!
How I love all of you for being what you are,
Neither good nor evil, too humble to be immoral,
Impervious to all progress,
Wondrous fauna from the depths of the sea of life!

(The donkey goes round and round
The water wheel in my yard,
And this is the measure of the world's mystery.

Wipe off your sweat with your arm, disgruntled worker.
The sunlight smothers the silence of the spheres
And we must all die,
O gloomy pine groves at twilight,
Pine groves where my childhood was different
From what I am today . . .)

Ah, but once more the incessant mechanical rage!
Once more the obsessive motion of buses.
And once more the fury of traveling in every train in the
    world
At the same time,
Of saying farewell from the deck of every ship
Which at this moment is weighing anchor or drawing away
    from a dock.
O iron, O steel, O aluminum, O corrugated sheet metal!
O wharfs, O ports, O trains, O cranes, O tugboats!

Hi-ya great train disasters!
Hi-ya caved-in mineshafts!
Hi-ya exquisite shipwrecks of great ocean liners!
Hi-ya-ho revolutions here, there and everywhere,
Constitutional changes, wars, treaties, invasions,
Outcries, injustice, violence, and perhaps very soon the end,
The great invasion of yellow barbarians across Europe,
And another Sun on the new Horizon!

But what does it matter? What does all this matter
To the glowing, red-hot racket of today,
To the delicious, cruel racket of modern civilization?
All this erases everything except the Moment,
The Moment with its bare chest as hot as a stoker's,
The shrill and mechanical Moment,
The dynamic Moment of all the bacchantes
Of iron and bronze and the drunk ecstasy of metals.

Hey trains, hey bridges, hey hotels at dinnertime,
Hey iron tools, heavy tools, minuscule and other tools,

Precision instruments, grinding tools, digging tools,
Mills, drills, and rotary devices!
Hey! hey! hey!
Hey electricity, Matter's aching nerves!
Hey wireless telegraphy, metallic sympathy of the
    Unconscious!
Hey tunnels, hey Panama, Kiel and Suez canals!
Hey all the past inside the present!
Hey all the future already inside us! Hey!
Hey! hey! hey!
Useful iron fruits of the cosmopolitan factory-tree!
Hey! hey! hey! Hey-ya-hi-ya!
I'm oblivious to my inward existence. I turn, I spin,
    I forge myself.
I'm coupled to every train.
I'm hoisted up on every dock.
I spin in the propellers of every ship.
Hey! hey-ya! hey!
Hey! I'm mechanical heat and electricity!
Hey! and the railways and engine rooms and Europe!
Hey and hooray for all in all and all in me, machines at
    work, hey!

To leap with everything over everything! Alley-oop!

Alley-oop, alley-oop, alley-oop-la, alley-oop!
Hey-ya, hi-ya! Ho-o-o-o-o!
Whir-r-r-r-r-r-r-r-r-r-r!

If only I could be every person and every place!

LONDON, JUNE 1914.

EXCERPTS FROM
TWO ODES

I

Come, ancient and unchanging Night,
Queen Night who was born dethroned,
Night inwardly equal to silence, Night
With sequin-stars that flicker
In your dress fringed by Infinity.

Come faintly,
Come softly,
Come alone, solemn, with hands hanging
At your sides, come
And bring the far-off hills as near as the nearby trees,
Merge every field I see into your one field,
Make the mountain one more block of your body,
Erase all its differences I see from afar,
All the roads that climb it,
All the varied trees that make it dark green in the distance,
All the white houses whose smoke rises through the trees,
And leave just a light here, a light there, another over there,
In the hazy and vaguely troubling distance,
In the distance that's suddenly impossible to cross.

Our Lady
Of the impossible things we seek in vain,
Of the dreams that come to us at dusk, by the window,
Of the plans that caress us
On sweeping terraces of cosmopolitan hotels

To the European sound of songs and voices near and far
And that pain us, for we know we'll never carry them out . . .

Come lull us,
Come cuddle us,
Kiss us softly on the forehead,
So gently on the forehead we wouldn't know we'd been
     kissed
Were it not for a slight change in our soul
And the hint of a sigh rising melodiously
From the most ancient part of us
In which are rooted all those wondrous trees
Whose fruits are the dreams we love and cherish
Because we know they have nothing to do with the things
     of life.

Come ever so solemnly,
Solemn and full
Of a secret desire to weep,
Perhaps because the soul is vast and life small,
And none of our gestures ever leaves our body,
And we can reach only as far as our arm reaches,
And can see only as far as our sight extends.

Come, ever sorrowful,
Mater Dolorosa of the Sufferings of the Meek,
Turris Eburnea of the Sorrows of the Scorned,
Cool hand on the feverish brow of the Humble,
Taste of water on the parched lips of the Weary.
Come out from the depths
Of the pale horizon,
Come pull me out
Of the soil of anxiety and barrenness
Where I thrive.
Pluck me, a forgotten daisy, from my soil.
Read in my petals I can't imagine what fortune
And strip them off to your satisfaction,
Your cool and quiet satisfaction.

Fling one of my petals to the North,
Home to the cities of Today I so loved.
Fling another of my petals to the South,
Home to the seas the Navigators first sailed.
Throw another petal Westward,
Where perhaps the entire Future glows red hot,
And I adore it even though it's unknown to me.
And throw another, the others, all that's left of me
To the East,
To the East from where everything comes, faith and the new
    day,
To the grandiose and fanatic and warm East,
To the extravagant East I'll never see,
To the Buddhist, Brahmanist, Shintoist East,
To the East which is everything we don't have,
Which is everything we're not,
To the East where—who knows?—perhaps Christ still lives,
Where perhaps God really exists and rules over all . . .

Come over the seas,
Over the widest seas,
Over the seas without definite horizons,
Come and pass your hand over the back of that wild, watery
    beast,
Mysteriously calming it,
O hypnotic tamer of greatly agitated things!

Come, ever considerate,
Come, ever maternal,
Come on tiptoe, ancient nurse who sat
At the bedside of the gods of now forgotten religions
And witnessed the birth of Jehovah and Jupiter
And smiled because for you all is false and useless.

Come, silent and ecstatic Night,
Come wrap your nocturnal white mantle
Around my heart,
Serenely like a breeze on a balmy afternoon,

Gently like a mother's soothing gesture,
With the stars shimmering in your hands
And the moon a mysterious mask on your face.
All sounds sound different
When you come.
All voices hush when you enter.
No one sees you enter.
No one knows when you have entered
Except of a sudden, when everything starts to withdraw,
When everything loses its edges and colors,
And high above, in the still bluish sky,
As a distinct crescent, a white circle, or just a sliver of
    new light,

The moon begins to be real.

II

Ah the twilight, nightfall, the lights turning on in big cities,
And the hand of mystery that stills the hubbub,
And the weariness of everything in us that hinders
An active and accurate feeling of Life!
Each street is a canal in a Venice of tediums,
And how mysterious the unanimous end of the streets
When the night falls, O my master Cesário Verde,
Who wrote "The Feeling of a Westerner"!

What profound restlessness, what longing for other things
That aren't countries or moments or lives!
What longing for perhaps other kinds of moods
Inwardly moistens this lingering, faraway moment!

A horror that sleepwalks among the city's first lights,
A tender and fluid terror that leans against street corners
Like a beggar waiting for impossible sensations
Without knowing who might bestow them . . .

When I die,
When I go away—ingloriously, like everyone—
Down that road whose very idea we can't face directly,
Through that door we'd never take if we could choose,
Toward that port unknown even to the captain of the Ship,
Let it be at this hour of day, worthy of all the tedium I've
    suffered,
This ancient and spiritual and mystical hour,
This hour in which perhaps, much longer ago than it seems,
Plato, dreaming, saw the idea of God
Shaping body and existence as something perfectly plausible
In his thoughts externalized like a field.

Let it be at this hour that you take me off to be buried,
At this hour when I don't know how to live,
When I don't know what to feel or pretend I feel,
At this hour whose mercy is tortured and excessive,
Whose shadows come from something other than things,
Whose passing drags no robes over the ground of
    Sensible Life
Nor leaves any fragrance on the paths of Sight.

Cross your hands on your knee, O consort I don't have or
    wish to have,
Cross your hands on your knee and look at me in silence
At this hour when I can't see that you're looking at me,
Look at me in silence and in secret, and ask yourself
—You who know me—who I am . . .

30 JUNE 1914

MARITIME ODE

Alone this summer morning on the deserted wharf,
I look toward the bar, I look toward the Indefinite,
I look and am glad to see
The tiny black figure of an incoming steamer.
It's still far away but distinct, classic in its own way.
It leaves a useless trail of smoke in the air far behind it.
It's coming in, and the morning with it, and here and there
Along the river maritime life begins to stir:
Sails are hoisted, tugboats advance,
Small boats jut out from behind the anchored ships.
There's a slight breeze.
But my soul is with what I least see,
The incoming steamer,
Because it's allied with Distance, with Morning,
With the maritime meaning of this Hour,
With the sweet pain that rises in me like a queasiness,
Like the onset of seasickness, but in my soul.

I look at the far-off steamer with great independence
    of mind,
And in me a flywheel slowly starts spinning.

The steamers coming in around the bar in the morning
Bring to my eyes
The happy and sad mystery of all who arrive and depart.
They bring memories of distant wharfs and other moments
Of another sort of the same humanity in other ports.
Every landing and every sailing of a ship

Is—I feel it in me like my own blood—
Unconsciously symbolic, terribly
Fraught with metaphysical meanings
That stir up in me the man I once was . . .

Ah, every wharf is a nostalgia made of stone!
And when the ship shoves off
And we suddenly notice a space widening
Between the wharf and the ship,
Then I'm hit by a fresh anxiety I can't explain,
A mist of sad feelings
Glistening in the sun of my grassy anxieties
Like the first dawn-lit window,
And it wraps me as if it were someone else's remembrance
Now mysteriously mine.

Ah, who knows, who knows
If I didn't already set sail from a wharf
A long time ago, before I ever was—if I, a ship
In the slanting light of dawn,
Didn't already depart from another kind of port?
Who knows if, long before the outer world as I know it
Dawned for me,
I didn't already depart
From a large wharf full of a few people,
From a large, half-awakened city,
From a huge, commercial, overgrown and apoplectic city,
As far as this is possible outside of Space and Time?

Yes, from a wharf, a wharf in some sense material,
Real, with the form of a wharf, a wharf in fact,
The Absolute Wharf whose model we've unconsciously
    imitated,
Unwittingly evoked, to build
Our wharfs that serve our ports,
Our wharfs of literal stone over actual water,
And once they're built they strike us without warning as
Real Things, Spirit Things, Soul-Stone Beings,

At certain moments of root feeling
When a door in the outer world seems to open
And, without anything changing,
Everything proves to be different.

Ah the Great Wharf from where we set sail in Nation-Ships!
O Great Primordial Wharf, eternal and divine!
Of what port? Over what waters? And why do I wonder?
Great Wharf like other wharfs, but the only One.
Buzzing, like them, with predawn silences
And blossoming with morning to the noise of cranes
And arriving freight trains,
Under an occasional, thin black cloud
Of smoke from nearby factories
That shades the black and shiny, coal-sprinkled ground
Like the shadow of a cloud passing over dusky waters . . .

Ah, what essence of mystery and senses arrested
In revelatory divine ecstasy
At hours colored by silence and anxieties
Forms the bridge between any wharf and The Wharf!

Wharf blackly reflected in still waters,
The bustle on board ships,
O wandering, restless soul of people who live in ships,
Of symbolic people who come and go, and for whom
    nothing lasts,
For when the ship returns to port
There's always some change on board!

O never-ending farewells, departures, inebriating
    Diversity!
Eternal soul of navigators and navigations!
Hulls slowly mirrored in the water
As the ship pulls out of port!
To float like life's soul, to sally forth like a voice,
To live the moment gently tossing on eternal waters,
To wake up to days more immediate than Europe's,

To see mysterious ports interrupting the sea's solitude,
To round far-off capes and find sudden vast landscapes
Of countless startled slopes . . .

Ah, the distant beaches, the wharfs seen from afar,
And then the beaches close up, the wharfs in plain view.
The mystery of every departure and every arrival,
The painful instability and inscrutability
Of this impossible universe
Felt more deeply in the skin with each passing maritime
    hour!
Our souls' absurd sobbing
Over unfamiliar ocean expanses with islands in the distance,
Over far-off coastlines of lands not visited,
Over the ports whose houses and people come into sharp relief
As the ship approaches.

Ah, how fresh the mornings of arrivals are,
And how pallid the mornings of departures,
When our insides tighten into a ball
And a vague sensation akin to fear
—The ancestral fear of leaving what we know and going away,
The mysterious ancestral fear of Arrival and the New—
Makes us shrink in our skin with anxiety.
And the whole of our anguished body, as if it were our soul,
Feels an inexplicable desire to feel all this
In some other way.
There's a nostalgia for something,
A stirring of affection, but for what uncertain country?
What coast? What ship? What wharf?
The thought languishes,
And we're left with a large inner void,
A hollow satiety of seaborne minutes,
And a vague anxiety that would be tedium or sorrow
If it knew how to be either . . .

Even so, the summer morning is slightly cool.
A slight torpor of night still wafts in the shaken air.

The flywheel in me spins a bit faster.
And the steamer is coming in, because I know it must be
    coming
 And not because I can see it moving at such a great distance.

In my imagination it's already close by and visible
All up and down its rows of portholes,
And everything in me trembles, all my muscles and flesh,
Because of that person who never arrives in any boat
And whom I've come to wait for today, because of an
    oblique command.

The ships coming in around the bar,
The ships setting out from ports,
The ships passing in the offing
(I imagine myself watching them from a deserted beach),
All these abstract ships about to depart—
All these ships move me as if they were more
Than mere ships, ships coming and going.

And ships seen from up close, even if we're not going to
    embark on them,
Seen from below, from the skiffs, next to the steel
    broadsides,
Seen from inside, in the cabins, the lounges, the galleys,
Seeing up close the masts tapering high overhead,
Brushing against the ropes, descending the cramped stairways,
Smelling the greasy metallic and maritime mixture of all
    this—
Ships seen from up close are something else and are the same,
Stirring the same nostalgia and the same yearning in
    another way.

The seafaring life! Everything it embraces and evokes!
All of its sweet seduction filters into my blood,
And I daydream indefinitely of voyages.
The distant coastlines, flattened by the horizon!
The capes, islands, and sandy beaches!

The maritime solitudes, like certain moments in the Pacific
When by the power of some suggestion learned in school
Our nerves feel the weight of its being the largest ocean,
And the world and the taste of things become a desert in us!
The more traveled, more human expanse of the Atlantic!
The Indian Ocean, the most mysterious of all!
And the Mediterranean, without mystery, soft and classical,
    a sea that washes
Esplanades eyed by white statues in nearby gardens!
How I'd love to hold all seas, all straits, all bays and all gulfs
Against my chest, feel them close, and die!

And you, O nautical things, my old dream toys!
Be my inner life, outside me!
Keels, masts and sails, helms, rigging,
Smokestacks, propellers, topsails, pennants,
Tiller ropes, hatchways, boilers, pipes and valves,
Fall inside of me in a heap, one big heap,
Like the jumbled contents of a drawer dumped out on the
    floor!
Be the treasure of my feverish greed,
Be the fruit of the tree of my imagination,
Theme of my songs, blood in the veins of my intellect,
The aesthetic link between me and the outside!
Provide me with metaphors, images, literature,
Because really and truly, seriously, literally,
My sensations are a boat with its keel in the air,
My imagination a half-sunken anchor,
My yearning a broken oar,
And the web of my nerves a net left to dry on the beach!

Somewhere on the river a single whistle blows.
The entire ground of my psyche is now trembling.
The flywheel in me keeps moving faster.

Ah, the steamers, the voyages, the not-knowing-the-
    whereabouts
Of so-and-so, a seaman of our acquaintance!

Ah, the glory of knowing that a man who fraternized
     with us
Was drowned off an island in the Pacific!
We who knew him will tell this to everyone
With all due pride and a quiet conviction
That all this has a broader and more beautiful meaning
Than just the loss of the ship on which he sailed
And his sinking to the bottom with his lungs full of water!

Ah, the steamers, the coal ships, the sailing ships!
How rare, alas! sailing ships are becoming on the high seas!
I who love modern civilization and kiss machines with all
     my soul,
I the engineer and sophisticate who studied abroad,
Would love to see once again only wooden ships and sailing
     vessels,
To know no other seafaring life besides the ancient life of the
     seas!
Because the ancient seas are Absolute Distance,
The Pure Faraway, free of the weight of Today . . .
Ah, how everything here reminds me of that better life,
Of those seas that were larger, since navigation was slower,
Of those seas that were mysterious, since no one knew much
     about them!

Every faraway steamer is a nearby sailing ship.
Every distant ship seen now is a ship from the past
     seen up close.
All the invisible sailors aboard ships on the horizon
Are visible sailors from the time of the old vessels,
From the slow, sail-driven age of perilous voyages,
From the wood and canvas age of voyages that took months.

The delirium of maritime things slowly takes hold of me,
The wharf and its atmosphere physically penetrate me,
The surging of the Tagus inundates my senses,
And I begin to dream, to be wrapped by the dream of the
     waters,

The transmission belts on my soul start turning hard,
And I'm visibly shaken by the flywheel's increasing speed.

The waters call me,
The oceans call me,
The faraway calls me with a bodily voice,
And it's every seafaring age there ever was, calling.

It was you, Jim Barnes, English sailor and my friend,
Who taught me that ancient English cry
Which so virulently sums up
For complex souls like mine
The confused call of the waters,
The uncanny, implicit voice of all maritime things,
Of shipwrecks, of long voyages, of dangerous crossings.
That English cry of yours, which in my blood becomes
    universal,
A cry like no other, without human form or voice,
That tremendous cry which seems to resound
Inside a cavern whose roof is the sky
And seems to tell all the sinister things
That can happen in the Faraway, on the Sea, at Night . . .
(You always pretended to be calling a schooner,
Cupping your large, dark and weathered hands
On the sides of your mouth to make a megaphone, crying:

Aho-o-o-o-o-o-o-o o-o-o- - - - yyyy . . .
Schooner aho-o-o-o-o-o-o-o-o-o-o-o-o- - - - yyyy . . .)

I can hear you from here, now, and I wake up to something.
The wind shudders. The morning rises. The heat sets in.
I feel my cheeks redden.
My conscious eyes dilate.
Ecstasy stirs, increases, ascends in me.
And with a blind, riotous hum
The flywheel's restless spinning accelerates.

O clamorous call
Whose heat and fury make all my yearnings

Seethe in one explosive ensemble,
And even my tediums—all of them!—become dynamic . . .
An appeal made to my blood
By an old love from I don't know where that returns
With still enough strength to allure and pull me,
With still enough power to make me hate this life
I live amidst the physical and psychic impermeability
Of the real people all around me!

Ah, to depart! By whatever means and to whatever place!
To set out across the waves, across unknown perils, across
    the sea!
To go Far, to go Wide, toward Abstract Distance,
Indefinitely, through deep and mysterious nights,
Carried like dust by the winds, by the gales!
To go, go, go once and for all!
All of my blood lusts for wings!
All of my body lurches forward!
I rush through my imagination in torrents!
I trample myself underfoot, I growl, I hurtle!
My yearnings burst into foam
And my flesh is a wave crashing into cliffs!

Thinking about this—O rage! Thinking about this—O fury!
Thinking about the smallness of my life full of yearnings,
Suddenly, tremulously, extraorbitally,
With a vicious, vast and violent rocking
Of the restless flywheel of my imagination,
The dark and sadistic estrus of the strident maritime life
Breaks out of me whistling, hooting, and raving.

Hey sailors, look-outs! Hey shipmates, pilots!
Navigators, seamen, mariners, adventurers!
Hey ship captains! Hey men at the helm and on the masts!
Men who sleep on wooden bunks!
Men who sleep with Danger peeking through the portholes!
Men who sleep with Death for a pillow!
Men who have decks and bridges from where they can gaze

Upon the vast vastness of the vast sea!
Hey crane operators!
Hey sail trimmers, stokers, cabin boys!
Men who load cargo in the holds!
Men who coil ropes on deck!
Men who polish the hardware of the hatches!
Men at the helm! men on the engines! men on the masts!
Hey-ey-ey-ey-ey-ey-ey!
Men with peaked caps! Men in mesh undershirts!
Men with anchors and crossed flags embroidered on their
    chests!
Tattooed men! Men with pipes! Men on the gunwales!
Swarthy from so much sun, shriveled from so much rain,
Clear-eyed from so much vastness all around them,
Bold-faced from so much wind having pounded them!
Hey-ey-ey-ey-ey-ey-ey!
Men who've seen Patagonia!
Men who've been to Australia!
Men who've feasted your eyes on coasts I'll never see!
Who've landed in lands where I'll never set foot!
Who bought primitive goods in colonies at the fore
    of hinterlands!
And you did all this as if it were nothing,
As if this were natural,
As if life were simply this,
As if you weren't even fulfilling a destiny!
Hey-ey-ey-ey-ey-ey-ey!
Men of today's ocean! Men of yesterday's ocean!
Pursers! Galley slaves! Combatants at Lepanto!
Pirates from Roman times! Mariners from Greece!
Phoenicians! Carthaginians! Portuguese launched from
    Sagres
Into an uncertain adventure, onto the Absolute Sea,
    to achieve the Impossible!
Hey-ey-ey-ey-ey-ey-ey-ey-ey!
Men who erected stone pillars and gave names to capes!
Men who traded for the first time with black people!
Who first sold slaves from new lands!

Who bestowed the first European spasm on startled Negro
   women!
Who brought back gold, beads, fragrant woods, arrows,
From hillsides bursting with lush vegetation!
Men who pillaged peaceful African villages,
Who put the natives to flight with booming cannons,
Who killed, who robbed, who tortured, who won
The reward of New Things for rushing headlong
Into the mystery of new seas! Hey-ey-ey-ey-ey!
I salute all of you in one man, and one man in all of you,
All of you mixed together, all intermingled,
All of you bloody, violent, hated, feared, fabled,
I salute you, I salute you, I salute you!
Hey-ey-ey-ey-ey! Hey-ey-ey-ey-ey! Hey-ey-ey-ey-ey-ey-ey!
Hey-la-oh-la-oh-la-OH-la-ah-ah-ah-ah-ah!

I want to go with you, I want to go with you,
With all of you at the same time
To every place you've been!
I want to meet head-on the same dangers you met,
To feel on my face the winds that withered yours,
To spit from my lips the salt of the seas that kissed yours,
To help swab your decks, to be with you in storms,
To arrive like you, finally, at extraordinary ports!
To flee with you from civilization!
To lose with you all sense of morality!
To feel my humanity change in faraway places.
To drink with you in southern seas
New savageries, new tumults in my soul,
New central fires in my volcanic spirit!
To go with you, to take off (Get the hell out of here!)
My civilized man's suit, my mild-mannered ways,
My congenital fear of chains and fetters,
My peaceful life,
My seated, static, orderly and repetitive life!

To the sea, the sea, the sea, the sea!
Ah, throw my life to the wind, to the waves,

To the sea!
Salt with windblown foam
My taste for great voyages!
Thrash with whipping water the flesh of my adventure,
Douse with the cold depths the bones of my existence,
Scourge, cut and shrivel with winds, foams and suns
My cyclonic, Atlantic being,
My nerves stretched out like taut shrouds,
A lyre in the hands of the winds!

Yes, yes, yes . . . Crucify me on your ocean crossings
And my shoulders will revel in my cross!
Tie me to your voyages as if to stakes,
And the sensation of the stakes will enter through my spine
And I'll feel them in a vast, passive ecstasy!
Do what you like with me, as long as it's at sea,
On ship decks, to the sound of waves.
Wound me, rip me open, kill me!
All I want is to take to Death
A soul overflowing with Sea,
Drunk silly on maritime things,
On sailors as well as on anchors, ropes,
On distant coasts as well as on the winds' howling,
On the Faraway as well as on the Wharf, on shipwrecks
As well as on peaceful trade operations,
On masts as well as on the waves,
To take to Death—in voluptuous pain—
A body covered with leeches sucking away,
Covered with strange, absurd, green sea leeches!

Make shrouds out of my veins!
Hawsers out of my muscles!
Flay my skin and nail it to the keels!
And let me feel the pain of the nails and never stop feeling it!
Make my heart into an admiral's flag
On a ship of old in time of war!
Yank out my eyes and grind them into the deck with your
    feet!

Smash my bones against the gunwales!
Tie me to the masts and thrash me, thrash me!
To all the winds of all latitudes and longitudes
Spill my blood over the raging waters
That sweep across the poop deck
In the storms' wild convulsions!

To have the audacity of sailcloth in the wind!
To be, like the topsails, the whistling of the winds!
An old guitar playing a fado about seas rife with dangers,
A song for sailors to hear and not repeat!

The mutinous sailors
Hung the captain from a sail yard.
Another they left on a desert isle,
Marooned!
The sun of the tropics has made my taut veins seethe
With the fever of old-time piracy.
The winds of Patagonia have tattooed my imagination
With tragic and obscene images.
Fire, fire, fire, inside me!
Blood! blood! blood! blood!
My brain is bursting!
The world as I know it explodes in red!
My veins snap with the sound of cables!
And from deep within booms the savage and insatiable
Song of the Great Pirate,
The bellowing death of the Great Pirate, whose singing
Sends a chill down the spine of his men.
Astern he dies, howling his song:

> *Fifteen men on the dead man's chest,*
> *Yo-ho-ho and a bottle of rum!*

And then yells in a blasting, unreal voice:

Darby M'Graw-aw-aw-aw-aw!
Darby M'Graw-aw-aw-aw-aw-aw-aw-aw!
Fetch a-a-aft the ru-u-u-u-u-u-u-u-um, Darby!

Ah, what a life! what a life that was!
Hey-ey-ey-ey-ey-ey-ey!
Hey-la-oh-la-oh-la-OH-la-ah-ah-ah-ah-ah!
Hey-ey-ey-ey-ey-ey-ey!

Split keels, sunken ships, blood on the seas!
Decks awash in blood, sectioned corpses!
Severed fingers left lying on gunwales!
Heads of children here and there!
People with gouged eyes shouting, screaming!
Hey-ey-ey-ey-ey-ey-ey-ey-ey!
Hey-ey-ey-ey-ey-ey-ey-ey!
I bundle up in all this as in a cloak when it's cold!
I rub against all this like a cat in heat against a wall!
I roar for all this like a famished lion!
I rush at all this like a crazed bull!
I dig my nails into this, break my claws on it and chew it till
    my teeth bleed!
Hey-ey-ey-ey-ey-ey-ey-ey-ey!

Suddenly I hear the old cry,
Now harsh, angry, metallic,
Like a bugle blasting at my side,
Calling the sighted prey,
The schooner that's going to be seized:

Aho-o-o-o-o-o-o-o-o-o-o- - - -yyyy . . .
Schooner aho-o-o-o-o-o-o-o-o-o-o-o-o-o- - - -yyyy . . .

The World has ceased to exist for me! I'm burning red!
I roar in fury for the attack!
Pirate chief! Pirate Caesar!
I plunder, kill, rip, slash!
All I feel is the sea, the prey, the pillage!
All I feel within are the veins of my temples
Beating, and beating me!
The sensation of my eyes is bleeding hot blood!
Hey-ey-ey-ey-ey-ey-ey-ey-ey!

Ah pirates, pirates, pirates!
Love me and hate me, pirates!
Take me into your midst, pirates!

How your rage and cruelty speak to the blood
Of a woman's body that once was mine and whose lust
    has survived!

I'd love to be an animal that would embody all your acts,
That would sink its teeth into the hulls and keels,
That would eat masts, drink blood and tar on ship decks,
Chew sails, oars, ropes and pulleys—
A monstrous, female sea-serpent gorging on your crimes!

And there's a symphony of incompatible and analogous
    sensations,
An orchestration in my blood of deafening crimes,
Of convulsive clamors from bloody orgies on the high sea,
All raging like a torrid gale through my mind,
A cloud of hot dust obscuring my perception
So that I see and dream all this with my skin and veins only!

Pirates, piracy, vessels and the hour,
The maritime hour when prey are captured
And the terror of the captured escapes into madness—
    that hour
With all its crimes, terror, vessels, people, sea, sky, clouds,
Breezes, latitude, longitude, shouting voices,
I'd like the Whole of this to be the Whole of my body,
    suffering,
To be my body and my blood, to form the stuff of my being
    in red,
To thrive like an itching wound in my soul's unreal flesh!

Ah, to be everything in every crime! To be all the component
    parts
Of raids on ships, of slaughters and rapes!
To be whatever was on the spot where pillages occurred,

To be whatever lived or was left dead on the site of
    gory tragedies!
To be the sum-total-pirate of all piracy at its zenith,
And the flesh-and-blood synthesis of all pirate victims in the
    world!

To be in my passive body every woman-all-women
Ever raped, killed, cut and mauled by pirates!
To be in my submissive self the female who needs to be
    theirs!
And to feel all this—all these things all at once—running
    down my spine!

O my hairy and gruff heroes of adventure and crime!
My seafaring brutes, husbands of my imagination!
Casual lovers of my oblique sensations!
I long to be That Woman who waits for you in ports,
For you, heinous men she loves in dreams with her pirate
    blood!
For she would rage with you, though only in spirit,
Over the naked corpses of your victims at sea!
For she would be with you in your crimes, and in your
    oceanic orgy
Her witch's spirit would invisibly dance around each
    movement
Of your bodies, your cutlasses, your strangling hands!
On land she would wait for you, and when you came, if you
    came,
In the howls of your loving she would drink all the vast,
Foggy and sinister perfume of your conquests,
And as you convulsed in ecstasy she would whistle a red and
    yellow sabbat!

Flesh torn, bodies cut open and gutted, the blood spurting!
Now as my dream of your deeds reaches its climax,
I lose myself completely, I stop belonging to you, I am you,
My femininity is not just to be with you, it's to be your very
    souls!

To be inside all your brutality at the time you wreaked it,
To imbibe deep down your consciousness of what you felt
When you tinged the high sea with blood,
When now and then you tossed to the sharks
The still living bodies of the wounded and the pink flesh of
    children,
And you dragged their mothers to the deck rails to look at
    what happened to them!

To be with you in your carnage and plundering!
To be harmonized with you in the symphony of your
    pillages!
Ah, how much and in how many ways I'd like to be yours!
To be not only your woman, not only your women, not only
    your victims,
Not only your victimized men, women, children and ships,
To be not only that hour and the vessels and the waves,
Not only your souls, your bodies, your rage, your spoils,
To be not only the abstract orgy of your deeds in my physical
    self,
Not only this, I'd like to be more than this—the God that's
    all this!
I'd have to be God, the God of an inverted faith,
A monstrous and satanic God, the God of a blood-based
    pantheism,
To be able to fill up every cranny of my imaginative fury
And still not exhaust my desire to identify
With each and every and more than every one of your
    conquests!

Ah, torture me to cure me!
Let my flesh be the air your cutlasses slice
Before they fall on heads and necks!
Let my veins be the clothes your knives rip right through!
My imagination the body of the women you rape!
My mind the deck you stand on while killing!
My entire life—in its nervous, hysterical, absurd ensemble—

The great organism in which every act of piracy ever committed
Would be a conscious cell, and all of me would spin
As a vast, waving rottenness, embodying all of this!

The feverish machine of my teeming visions
Now spins at such frightening, inordinate speed
That my flywheel consciousness
Is just a blurry circle whirring in the air.

> *Fifteen men on the dead man's chest,*
> *Yo-ho-ho and a bottle of rum!*

Hey-la-oh-la-oh-la-OH- - - - la-ah-ah-ah-ah-ah- - - - ah-ah-ah . . .

Ah! the savagery of this savagery! To hell
With every life like ours, which has none of this!
Look at me: an engineer! Necessarily practical, sensitive to
   everything,
Static in comparison to you, even when I walk;
Inert, even when I act; weak, even when I assert myself;
Stagnant, shattered, a fainthearted renegade of your Glory,
Of your shrill, hot and bloody dynamic!

Damn my inability to turn my delirium into action!
Damn my always hanging on to civilization's apron strings!
Damn the dainty manners I carry on my back like a bale of
   lace!
Errand boys of modern humanitarianism—that's what we
   all are!
A sorry lot of consumptives, neurasthenics, and phlegmatics,
Without the courage to be violent and daring men,
Our souls tied up like a chicken by the leg!

Ah, pirates! pirates!
The yearning for lawlessness coupled with brutality,
The yearning for absolutely cruel and abominable things,
Gnawing like an abstract lust at our delicate bodies,

At our squeamish and effeminate nerves,
And bringing mad fevers into our empty gazes!

Make me kneel down before you!
Beat and humiliate me!
Make me your slave and your plaything!
And don't ever deprive me of your contempt!
O my masters! O my lords!

To always gloriously take the submissive part
In bloody deeds and protracted sensualities!
Fall on me like massive walls,
O barbarians of the ancient sea!
Rip me and wound me!
Streak my body with blood
From east to west!
Kiss with cutlasses, whips and rage
My blissful carnal fear of belonging to you,
My masochistic yearning to submit to your fury,
To be the sentient, impassive object of your omnivorous
    cruelty,
Rulers, lords, emperors, steeds!
Ah, torture me,
Rip me apart!
And once I've been hacked into conscious pieces,
Strew me over the decks,
Scatter me across the waters, leave me
On the voracious beaches of islands!

Satiate in me all my mysticism of you!
Engrave my soul in blood!
Cut and slash!
O tattooers of my bodily imagination!
Beloved flayers of my fleshly submission!
Subdue me like a dog that's kicked to death!
Make me the vessel of your lordly disdain!

Make me all your victims!
As Christ suffered for all men, I want to suffer

For all who've been victims at your hands,
Your callused and bloody hands, with fingers lopped off
In sudden attacks at the gunwales!

Make me into something that's dragged
—Oh what pleasure, oh what delicious pain!—
As if behind horses whipped by you ...
But all this at sea, at se-e-e-ea, at SE-E-E-EA!
Hey-ey-ey-ey-ey! Hey-ey-ey-ey-ey-ey-ey! HEY-EY-EY-EY-
     EY-EY-EY! At S-E-E-E-EA!
Yey-ey-ey-ey-ey-ey! Yey-ey-ey-ey-ey-ey! Yey-ey-ey-ey-ey-ey-
     ey-ey!
Everything shouts out! Every last thing shouts! Winds, waves,
     boats,
Seas, topsails, pirates, my heart, blood, and the air, the air!
Hey-ey-ey-ey-ey! Yey-ey-ey-ey-ey! Yey-ey-ey-ey-ey-ey! Everything
     shouts out in song!

             FIFTEEN MEN ON THE DEAD MAN'S CHEST.
             YO-HO-HO AND A BOTTLE OF RUM!

Hey-ey-ey-ey-ey-ey-ey! Hey-ey-ey-ey-ey-ey-ey! Hey-ey-ey-ey-
     ey-ey-ey!
Hey-la-oh-la-oh-la-OH-O-O-o-o-la-ah-ah-ah- - - - ah-ah-ah!

AHO-O-O-O-O-O-O-O-O-O-O- - -yyy! . . .
SCHOONER AHO-O-O-O-O-O-O-O-O-O- - - -yyy! . . .

Darby M'Graw-aw-aw-aw-aw-aw!
DARBY M'GRAW-AW-AW-AW-AW-AW-AW!
FETCH A-A-AFT THE RU-U-U-U-U-UM, DARBY!

Hey-ey-ey-ey-ey-ey-ey-ey-ey-ey-ey-ey!
HEY-EY-EY-EY-EY-EY-EY-EY-EY-EY-EY-EY!
HEY-EY-EY-EY-EY-EY-EY-EY-EY-EY-EY-EY!
HEY-EY-EY-EY-EY-EY-EY-EY-EY-EY-EY-EY!

HEY-EY-EY-EY-EY-EY-EY-EY-EY-EY-EY-EY!

Something in me snaps. The red has darkened into night.
I felt too much to be able to keep on feeling.
My soul is spent, only an echo in me remains.
The flywheel is slowing down.
My dreams lift their hands a bit from my eyes.
There's nothing in me but a void, a desert, a nocturnal sea.
And as soon as I feel this nocturnal sea in me,
Then again, yet again, from out of the silence
Of its endless distance, the vast and age-old cry arises.
Like a lightning flash of sound—soothing, not noisy—
Suddenly encompassing all the watery maritime
Horizon and dark human surging in the night,
Like the voice of a distant siren weeping, calling, it rises
From the depths of the Far, the depths of the Sea, the heart
    of all Abysses,
And on the surface, like seaweed, float my broken
    dreams . . .

Aho-o-o-o-o-o-o-o-o-o-o- - - -yy . . .
Schooner aho-o-o-o-o-o-o-o-o-o-o-o-o- - - -yy . . .

Ah, the freshness of dew on my exhilaration!
The coolness of night on my inner ocean!
Everything in me suddenly beholds a night at sea
Full of the vast and utterly human mystery of the nocturnal
    waves.
The moon rises on the horizon
And my happy childhood wells up in me like a tear.
My past resurfaces, as if that mariner's cry
Were a scent, a voice, the echo of a song
Calling up from my past
That happiness I'll never again know.

It was in the old peaceful house by the river . . .
(My bedroom windows, like the dining room windows,
Looked out over some low-lying houses and, just beyond
    them, the river,
The Tagus, this very same Tagus but at a point further down.

If today I gazed out the same windows, I wouldn't gaze out
   the same windows.
That time has passed like smoke from a steamer on the high
   sea . . .)

· An inexplicable feeling of tenderness,
A tearful and heartfelt remorse,
For all those victims—especially the children—
I dreamed of hurting when I dreamed I was a pirate of
   old . . .
A feeling of regret, since they were my victims;
A soft and tender feeling, since they weren't really.
A confused emotion, bluish like a fogged window,
Sings old songs in my poor grieving heart.

Ah, how could I think or dream those things?
How far I am from what I was a few minutes ago!
What hysterical feelings—first one thing, then the opposite!
As the blond morning rises, my ears prefer to hear only
Things that concur with this emotion—the lapping of
   the waters,
The river water's gentle lapping against the wharf . . . ,
The sailboat passing along the river's far shore,
The distant, Japanese-blue hills,
The houses of Almada,
And whatever's soft and childlike in the early morning
   hours! . . .

A seagull passes by
And my tenderness increases.

But all this time I wasn't paying any attention.
All those things I felt were only skin-deep, like a caress.
All this time I never took my eyes off my distant dream,
My house by the river,
My childhood by the river,
My bedroom windows looking out onto the river at night,
And the peace of the moonlight scattered over the waters!

My old aunt, who loved me because of the son she'd lost . . .
My old aunt used to sing me to sleep
(Even though I was already too old for this).
The memory makes tears fall on my heart, cleansing it
    of life,
And a light sea breeze wafts inside me.
Sometimes she sang "The Good Ship Catrineta":

> *There goes the Catrineta*
> *Over the waves of the sea . . .*

And at other times it was "The Fair Princess," with its
    wistful,
Medieval melody . . . I recall this, and her poor old voice
    rises in me,
Reminding me how little I've thought of her since then, and
    she loved me so much!
How ungrateful I've been to her—and what have I done with
    my life?
Yes, "The Fair Princess" . . . I'd close my eyes as she sang:

> *The Fair Princess*
> *Sat in her garden . . .*

And I'd open my eyes just a sliver, see the window full
    of moonlight,
And shut them again, and in these moments I was happy.

> *The Fair Princess*
> *Sat in her garden*
> *Combing her hair*
> *With her golden comb . . .*

O my childhood days, a doll someone broke!

If I could only go back in time, to that house and that
    affection,
And remain there forever, forever a child and forever
    happy!

But all of this is the Past, a lantern on an old street corner.
Remembering it makes me cold, and hungry for something
    unobtainable.
Thinking of it stirs in me an absurd regret for I don't
    know what.
O slow whirlpool of conflicting sensations!
Faint vertigo of confused things in my soul!
Shattered furies, tender feelings like spools of thread children
    play with,
Avalanches of imagination over the eyes of my senses,
Tears, useless tears,
Light breezes of contradiction grazing the face of my
    soul . . .

To shake off this emotion, I invoke with a conscious effort,
I invoke with a desperate, worthless, arid effort
The song of the Great Pirate as he was dying:

> *Fifteen men on the dead man's chest,*
> *Yo-ho-ho and a bottle of rum!*

But the song is a straight line drawn crookedly inside me . . .

With a struggle I'm able, but through an almost literary
    imagination,
To bring back into my soul's field of vision
The rage of piracy, of slaughter, the almost mouth-watering
    appetite for pillage,
For the frivolous slaughter of women and children,
For the gratuitous torture of the poor passengers, merely to
    amuse ourselves,
And the sensuality of breaking and shattering the things
    others most cherish,
But I dream all this while dreading something breathing
    down my neck.

I remember how interesting it would be
To hang sons before their mothers' eyes

(But I can't help but feel like the mothers),
To bury alive four-year-old children on desert isles,
Taking their parents there in boats to see
(But I shudder, remembering the son I don't have who's
    quietly sleeping at home).

I try to stir a dead yearning for sea crimes,
For an inquisition without the excuse of Faith,
Crimes without even any wrath or malice behind them,
Carried out mechanically, not to hurt, not to harm
And not even to amuse ourselves, but just to pass
    the time,
Like country people who play solitaire at the dining table
    after dinner, with the tablecloth pushed to one side,
Just for the soothing pleasure of committing heinous crimes
    and thinking nothing of it,
Of watching suffering victims reach the brink of madness
    and death-from-pain without letting them cross it . . .
But my imagination refuses to go along.
A shiver runs through me.
And suddenly, more suddenly than before, from farther away
    and deeper down,
Suddenly—oh the terror coursing through my veins!
Oh the sudden cold from the door to Mystery that opened
    in me and let in a draft!—
I remember God, the Transcendent in life, and suddenly
The old voice of the English sailor Jim Barnes, whom I used
    to talk with,
Becomes in me the voice of my mysterious affection for silly
    things like a mother's lap and a sister's hair ribbon,
A voice arriving miraculously from beyond the appearance
    of things,
The faint and remote Voice that's now the Absolute Voice,
    the Mouthless Voice,
Arriving from above and from within the seas' nocturnal
    solitude,
Calling me, calling me, calling me . . .

It comes faintly, as if muffled but still audible,
From far away, almost too far away to be heard from here,
Like a stifled sob, a snuffed flame, a silent breath,
From no corner in space, from no place in time,
The eternal cry of night, a deep and confused murmur:

Aho-o-o-o-o-o-o-o-o-o-o-o---yyy . . . . . .
Aho-o-o-o-o-o-o-o-o-o-o-o-o-o-o----yyy . . . .
Schooner aho-o-o-o-o-o-o-o-o-o-o-o-o-o-o-o-----yy . . . . . .

A cold chill from the soul makes my whole body shiver,
And I suddenly open my eyes, which I hadn't closed.
Ah, what joy to emerge once and for all from my dreams!
To return to the real world, so easy on the nerves!
The world on this early morning when the day's first
    steamers are arriving . . .

I've lost interest in that incoming steamer that's still far
    away.
Now only what's close to me cleanses my soul.
My healthy, rugged, pragmatic imagination
Is concerned now only with useful, modern things,
With freighters, steamers and passengers,
With rugged, immediate, modern, commercial, real things.
The flywheel in me is slowing down.

Wonderful modern maritime life—
Clean, fit, and full of machines!
All so well ordered, so spontaneously organized,
All the machine parts, all oceangoing vessels,
All aspects of import and export trade activity
So perfectly integrated
That everything seems to happen by natural laws,
Nothing ever colliding with anything else!

Nothing has lost its poetry. And now there are also machines
With their poetry, and this entirely new kind of life,
This commercial, worldly, intellectual and sentimental life

Which the machine age has conferred on our souls.
Voyages are as lovely as they ever were,
And a ship will always be lovely, just because it is a ship.
Travel is still travel, and the faraway is where it has
    always been:
Nowhere at all, thank God!

The ports full of every kind of steamer!
Large and small, of various colors, their portholes variously
    arranged,
And belonging to so wonderfully many shipping lines!
Steamers in port, so individual in their clearly demarcated
    berths!
So attractive in their stately calm of commercial things that
    ply the sea,
The ancient and forever Homeric sea, O Ulysses!
The humanitarian glance of lighthouses far off in the night!
Or the sudden flashing of a nearby lighthouse on a dark
    dark night
("How close we were to the coast!" And the sound of the
    water sings in our ear!) . . .

All this is as it always was, but today there's commerce,
And the commercial destiny of the great steamers
Makes me proud of my era!
The variety of people aboard passenger ships
Fills me with the modern pride of living at a time when it's
    so easy
For races to mix together and distances to be crossed, so easy
    to see everything
And enjoy life, making a good number of dreams come true.

Neat, orderly and modern like an office with service
    windows made of latticed yellow wire,
My present feelings—natural and sober like gentlemen—
Are practical and free of hysteria, filling their lungs with
    ocean air
Like people perfectly aware of how healthy it is to breathe
    air from the sea.

The day's working hours have now definitely commenced.
Everything begins to move, to get organized.

With immense and natural pleasure I follow with my soul
All the commercial operations needed for a shipment of
    goods.
My era is the rubber stamp appearing on all invoices,
And I feel that all letters from all offices
Should be addressed to me.

A bill of lading is so distinctive,
And a ship captain's signature so handsome and modern!
The commercial formality at the beginning and end of letters:
Dear Sirs—Messieurs—Amigos e Senhores,
Yours faithfully—Nos salutations empressées . . .
All of this isn't only human and tidy but also beautiful,
And it ultimately has a maritime destiny: a steamer on which
    are loaded
The goods named in the letters and invoices.

Life's complexity! Though drawn up by people
Who love, hate, have political passions and sometimes
    commit crimes,
The invoices are so neat, so well written, so independent of
    all that!
Some people look at an invoice and don't feel this.
Surely you felt it, Cesário Verde.
And I feel it so humanly it makes me cry.
Don't try to tell me there's no poetry in business and in offices!
It enters through every pore . . . I breathe it in this ocean air,
Because all of this concerns steamers and modern navigation,
Because invoices and business letters are the beginning of the
    story,
And the ships carrying the goods across the eternal sea are
    the end.

Ah, and the voyages—holiday voyages and other kinds . . .
Voyages on the sea, where we're all companions

In a special way, as if a maritime mystery
Brought our souls together and transformed us for a
     moment
Into transient citizens of the same uncertain country,
Eternally moving over the vastness of the waters!
Grand hotels of the Infinite, O my transatlantic ships!
Totally and perfectly cosmopolitan, for you never stay long
     in one place,
And you contain every sort of face, costume and race!

Voyages, voyagers—so many different kinds!
So many nationalities, professions and people in the world!
So many different directions one can take in life,
In this life which at heart is always, always the same life!
So many curious faces! All faces are curious,
And nothing makes for holiness like constantly looking at
     people.
Brotherhood is not after all a revolutionary idea.
It's something we learn in daily life, where everything has to
     be tolerated.
And we begin to appreciate what we have to tolerate,
Until we nearly weep with affection for what we once
     tolerated!

Ah, all this is beautiful, all this is human and linked
To human feelings, so sociable and bourgeois,
So complexly simple, so metaphysically sad!
The diversified, floating life ends up educating us in
     humanity.
Poor humans! Poor humans all of us!

I take leave of this moment in the person of this other ship
Which is now setting sail. It's an English tramp steamer,
Very dirty, as if it were a French ship,
With the friendly air of a seaborne proletarian,
And no doubt mentioned on the back page of yesterday's
     papers.

My heart goes out to the poor steamer, so humble and
   unassuming.
It seems to feel responsible for something, to be an honest
   person,
Faithful to some duty or other.
There it goes, leaving me behind on this wharf.
There it goes, placidly passing where sailing ships once
   passed,
Long, long ago . . .
To Cardiff? Liverpool? London? It doesn't matter.
It does its duty. As we should do ours. Marvelous life!
Bon voyage! Bon voyage!
Bon voyage, my poor chance friend who did me the favor
Of taking with you the sadness and delirium of my dreams,
Restoring me to life so I can watch you and see you sail
   away.
Bon voyage! Bon voyage! That's what life is . . .
With what natural elegance so typical of morning
You sail tall and straight from out of Lisbon's harbor today!
I feel strangely endeared and grateful to you for this . . .
For this what? Who knows what! . . . Go on . . . Sail
   away . . .
With a slight quiver
(Tch-tch- -tch- - -tch- - - -tch- - - - -tch . . .)
The flywheel in me comes to a halt.

Sail away, slow steamer, sail and don't stay . . .
Sail away from me, sail out of my sight,
Depart from inside my heart,
Disappear into the Faraway, the Faraway, the mist of God,
Disappear, follow your destiny and leave me . . .
Who am I to weep for you and question you?
Who am I to speak to you and love you?
Who am I to be troubled by the sight of you?
It pushes off from the wharf, the sun rises golden, shines
   brighter,
 Glancing off the rooftops of the buildings on the wharf.

The whole of this side of the city is gleaming . . .
Depart, leave me, become
First the ship in mid-river, clear and unmistakable,
Then a small, black ship headed toward the bar,
Then a hazy point on the horizon (O anxiety!),
An ever hazier point on the horizon . . .
Then nothing, just me and my sadness,
And the great city now bathed in sunlight,
And the real, naked hour like a wharf without ships,
And the slow turning of the crane, like a turning compass,
Tracing a semicircle of I don't know what emotion
In the staggered silence of my soul . . .

[1915]

SALUTATION TO
WALT WHITMAN

Portugal, Infinity—June eleventh, nineteen hundred and
    fifteen . . .
Hey-la-a-a-a-a-a-a!

From here in Portugal, with every historical age in my brain,
I salute you, Walt, I salute you, my Universal brother,
Forever modern and eternal, the singer of concrete
    absolutes,
Passionate mistress of the scattered universe,
Great homosexual who rubs against the diversity of things,
Sexualized by stones, by trees, by people, by professions,
Full of lust for passing bodies, chance encounters, mere
    observations,
Champion of the material substance of all things,
My glorious hero who goes into Death skipping,
Greeting God with shouts and roars and squeals!

Singer of fierce and tender brotherhood with all things,
Great democrat in all your pores, close in body and soul to
    everything,
Carnival of all actions, bacchanalia of all intentions,
Twin brother of all initiatives,
Jean-Jacques Rousseau of the world bound to produce
    machines,
Homer of the elusive carnal flux,
Shakespeare of sensations that were beginning to run on
    steam,
Milton-Shelley of Electricity on the horizon!

Incubus of all gestures,
Inner spasm of all outer objects,
Pimp of the whole Universe,
Slut of all solar systems, pansy of God!

I, with my monocle and exaggeratedly tight-waisted coat,
Am not unworthy of you, Walt, and you know it.
I'm not unworthy of you, for the simple reason that I salute
     you . . .
I, so prone to inertia and so easily bored,
Am one of yours, you know I am, and I love and understand
     you,
And although I never met you, being born around the year
     you died,
I know you loved me too, you knew me, and it gladdens my
     heart.
I know that you knew me, considered me and explained me,
And I know that that's what I am, whether on the Brooklyn
     Ferry ten years before I was born
Or on the Rua do Ouro today, thinking about everything
     that's not the Rua do Ouro,
And as you felt everything, I feel everything, we walk hand
     in hand,
Hand in hand, Walt, hand in hand, dancing the universe in
     our soul.

I kiss your picture all the time.
Wherever you are now (I don't know where, but I know it's
     God)
You feel this, I know you feel it, and my kisses (in person)
     are warmer,
Which is how you want them, and so you thank me from
     where you are,
I'm sure of it, something tells me so—a satisfied feeling in
     my spirit,
An indirect, abstract erection in the depths of my soul.
You were cyclopean and muscular, not pretty,
Yet your attitude toward the world was feminine,

And for you each leaf of grass, each stone and each person
    was the Universe.

Here's to you, dear old Walt, my great Comrade, evoe!
I belong to your Bacchic orgy of sensations-in-freedom,
I'm one of yours—from the feeling in my feet to the nausea
    in my dreams.
I'm one of yours, look at me. From where you are, in God,
    you see me in reverse,
From inside out . . . You divine my body; what you see is my
    soul,
Seeing it directly, and through its eyes my body.
Look at me: you know that I, Álvaro de Campos, engineer,
Sensationist poet,
Am not your disciple, not your lover, and not your singer.
You know I'm You and are glad for it!

I can never read much of your poetry at once . . . It's too full
    of feeling . . .
I move through your verses as through a jostling crowd,
And they smell to me of sweat, of oil, of human and
    mechanical activity,
So that I finally don't know if I'm reading or living,
I don't know if my true place is in the world or in your
    poetry,
I don't know if I'm here, with both feet on the natural earth,
Or if I'm hanging upside down in some sort of emporium,
Dangling from the natural ceiling of your tumultuous
    inspiration,
From the middle of the ceiling of your unattainable intensity.

Open all the doors!
I'm coming through!
My password? Walt Whitman!
But to hell with a password . . .
I'll just come on through . . .
I'll break down the doors if I have to . . .
Yes, I who am meek and civilized will break down the doors,

Because in this moment I'm not meek or civilized,
I'm ME, a thinking universe of flesh and blood that wants to
    get through
And that *will* get through, for when I want to get through,
    I'm God!

Get this rubbish out of my sight!
Stash these emotions into drawers!
Away with politicians, literati,
Staid businessmen, policemen, prostitutes, pimps!
All of this is the letter that kills, not the spirit that gives life.
The spirit that gives life in this moment is ME!

Let no son of a bitch cross my path!
My path is through infinity all the way to the end!
Whether or not I can reach the end is none of your business,
    let me go,
It concerns only me, and God, and the meaning-that's-me of
    the word Infinite . . .
Forward!
I dig in the spurs!
And I feel the spurs, I'm the selfsame horse I ride,
Because I, through my will to be one with God,
Can be everything, or nothing, or anything,
Depending on my mood . . . It's no one else's business . . .
Raging delirium! I want to yelp, to leap,
To rant, rave, jump, twirl and shout with my body,
To cling to car wheels and get rolled over,
To lie beneath the twisting of the whip that's going to
    crack . . . . .
To be the she-dog of all he-dogs and still not be satisfied,
To be the flywheel of all machines and never go fast
    enough,
To be whatever's crushed, abandoned, uprooted, destroyed,
And all for you, to sing and salute you . . . . .
Dance with me this delirium, Walt, in the world where you
    are now,
Hop with me in this tribal dance that bumps into the stars,

Fall with me to the ground from exhaustion,
Dash with me into the walls until we're dazed,
Shatter with me into smithereens . . . . .
In all, through all, around all, without all,
An abstract bodily rage stirring maelstroms in the soul . . .

Come on! Forward!
Even if God tries to stop us, let's go forward . . . It doesn't
    matter . . .
Let's go forward,
Forward, to no place at all . . .
Infinity! The Universe! Goal with no goal! What does it
    matter?
Boom! boom! boom! boom! boom!
Right now, yes, let's go, straight ahead, boom!
Boom!
Boom!
Hup-hup . . . hup-hup . . . hup-hup . . . hup-hup . . .

Like a hurled thunderbolt I rush
Toward you in leaps of the heart.
With military bands leading the way, I keep saluting you . . .
In a grand procession with frenzied shouting and jumping
I scream out your name at the top of my lungs,
And every cheer for me and for you and for God I give to
    you,
And the universe spins around us like a carousel with music
    inside our heads,
And I, with intrinsic lights in my anterior epidermis,
Mad from the drunken, musical hissing of machines,
And you, the renowned, the reckless, you (. . .)

◆

And so it's to you I address
My verses that are leaps, my verses that are jumps, my
    spasm verses,
My hysterical-attack verses,
My verses that pull the carriage of my nerves.

Tripping and stumbling I get inspired,
I'm so excited I can hardly breathe or stand still,
And my verses are my not being able to burst from living.

Throw open all the windows!
Rip all the doors off their hinges!
Pull the house down on top of me!
I want to live at large in the open air,
I want to have gestures outside my body,
I want to run like rain down the walls,
I want to be stepped on like the paving stones of roadways,
I want to sink like a dead weight to the bottom of the sea,
With a sensuality I lost ages ago!

I don't want any latches on doors!
I don't want any locks on coffers!
I want to mix in, to merge, to be swept along,
I want to become someone else's aching possession,
To be dumped out of garbage cans,
To be tossed into the sea,
To be sought out at home for obscene purposes—
Anything but to keep on sitting here quietly!
Anything but to keep on writing these verses!

I want a world without gaps!
I want objects to materially touch and penetrate each
    other!
I want physical bodies to belong to each other like souls,
Not just dynamically but statically too!

I want to fly and to fall from high up!
To be hurled like a grenade!
To end up in X, to be taken to Y . . .
Abstract apogee at the end of me and of everything!

Motorized iron climax!
Stairless staircase of speed climbing higher!

Hydraulic pump extracting my throbbing guts like an
    anchor!

Put me in shackles just so that I can break them!
So that I can break them with my teeth and make my teeth
    bleed!
O masochistic, blood-spurting joy of life!

The sailors took me prisoner.
Their hands squeezed me in the darkness,
And I died for a moment when I felt this.
Then my soul licked the floor of my private jail
To the buzzing of impossibilities drowning out my protests.

Leap, jump, bite down on the bit,
Red-hot Pegasus of my restless yearnings,
Uncertain end of my motorized destiny!
Jump, leap, drape yourself with flags,
Mark the nocturnal vastness with your trail in blood,
In hot blood stretching far behind you,
In fresh blood stretching far behind you,
In cold, living blood through the air I dynamically feel!
Jump, hurdle, leap,
Alley-oop, keep jumping . . . . .

◆

My cavalcade-prayer!
My forward charge-salutation!

Who besides you felt the individual life in each thing?
Who besides you felt himself, and life and us
    to exhaustion?
Who besides you always preferred the spare part to the
    regular one
And made it his norm to violate Life's norms and
    forms?
    . . . . .

My happiness is a rage,
My forward charge a collision
    (Bam!)
In me . . .

In you, O Master of my healthful disease,
I salute the first classic case of universalitis,
The "Whitman syndrome," which is what afflicts me!
St. Walt of Shrieking Deliriums and Rage!

◆

Gateway to everything!
Bridge to everything!
Road to everything!
Your omnivorous soul . . . . .
Your soul that's bird, fish, beast, man, woman,
Your soul the two where there are two,
Your soul the one that's two where two are one.
Your soul that's arrow, lightning, space,
Embrace, nexus, sex, Texas, Carolina, New York,
Brooklyn Ferry in the evening,
Brooklyn Ferry coming and going,
Libertad! Democracy! The twentieth century up ahead!
Boom! boom! boom! boom! boom!
BOOM!

You, what you were, what you saw, what you heard,
Subject and object, active and passive,
Here and there, everywhere you,
A circle encompassing all ways of feeling,
Milestone of all things possible,
God-Boundary of all objects imaginable—that's you!
You the Hour,
You the Minute,
You the Second!
You interspersed, liberated, unfurled, departed,
Interspersion, liberation, departure, unfurlment,
Intersperser, liberator, unfurler, sender,

Postmark on all letters,
Name in all addresses,
Merchandise delivered, returned, in transit . . .
Train of sensations moving at soul-miles per hour,
Per hour, per minute, per second. BOOM!

And all these natural, human and mechanical noises
Go together, a sum tumult of everything,
Full of me to you, saluting you—
Human shouts and earthly cries,
Echoes from hills,
The burbling of waters,
The loud blasts of war,
The roaring of beasts in the distance,
The muffled sounds of sighs in the darkness.
And closer to life, surrounding me
(And it's my finest prize for saluting you),
There are the whistles, chugging and screeching of trains,
The modern noises, factory noises,
Steady hum,
Motor wheels,
Flywheels,
Propellers
Boom . . .

◆

In a great all-cities-of-Europe *marche aux flambeaux*,
In a great war march of industry, commerce and leisure,
In a great race, in a great rise, in a great fall,
Howling, jumping, and everything jumping with me,
I leap up and salute you,
I salute you with loud shouts,
I salute you with a burst of somersaults, handstands and
    hoorays!
Hey-la!
(. . .)

◆

Hey-la, I'm going to summon
All the human swarming of the Universe,
All varieties of all emotions,
All types of all thoughts,
All wheels, all gears and all pistons of the soul
To the blaring, deafening privilege of saluting you.
Hup-hup! I shout,
And in a procession of Me to you they all rumble
In a metaphysical and real gibberish,
In an uproar of things clashing within me . . . . .

Ave, hail, hurrah, O great bastard of Apollo,
Passionate, impotent lover of the nine Muses and three
      Graces,
Funicular from Olympus to us and from us to Olympus,
Rage of the modern materialized in me,
Transparent spasm of being,
Flower of other people's actions,
Joyous feasting because there's Life,
Mad fury because no one has enough life to be all people,
Since being means being limited, and only God could
      satisfy us.
Ah, you sang everything and yet left everything unsung.
Who can include more than their body in their body?
Or feel more feelings than there are to feel?
Who can be sufficient when nothing suffices?
Who can be complete as long as one blade of grass
Has its root outside their heart?

◆

Open all the doors!
Break all the windows!
Remove the locks from this enclosing life!
Remove this enclosing life from this enclosing life!
Let closing be openness, with no locks as reminders,
Let "stopping" be the ignorant term for continuing,
Let the end be an always abstract thing,
Fluidly connected to every hour that passes by it.

I want to breathe!
Strip my body of all its weight!
Replace my soul with abstract wings attached to nothing!
No, not wings, just the enormous Wing of Flight itself!
No, not even Flight, just the speed that remains when flying
    is flying
And there's no body to weigh down the soul of Going!

I want to be the heat of living things, the fever
Of saps, the rhythm of waves and the . . . . .
Gap in Being that allows Being to be . . . !

No boundaries anywhere!
No divisions in anything!
Just Me.

◆

Where I'm not the first, I prefer to be nothing, to not be
    there.
Where I can't be the first to act, I prefer to watch others act.
Where I can't rule, I refuse even to obey.

I ardently yearn for everything, so ardently that I never miss
    out,
And I don't miss out because I don't try.
"All or nothing" has a special meaning for me.
But I can't be universal, because I'm individual.
I can't be everybody, because I'm One, just one, just me.
I can't be first in anything, because there is no first.
And so I prefer the nothing of being nothing but that
    nothing.

When does the last train leave, Walt?
I want to leave this city known as Earth,
I want to emigrate from the country of Me once and for all,
To leave the world like a man who admits defeat,
Like a traveling salesman who sells ships to people from the
    interior.

To the junk heap with broken motors!
What was my entire being? An enormous, useless yearning,
A sterile pursuit of an impossible goal,
A madman's machine to achieve perpetual motion,
A crackpot theorem to prove that a circle is square,
An attempt to swim across the Atlantic that failed
Before I ever entered the water, just by looking at it and
    calculating,
A hail of stones at the moon,
An absurd desire for the two parallels of God and life to
    meet.

My nerves' megalomania,
My rigid body's yearning for elasticity,
My physical self's rage because it's not the sovereign axis,
The sensual vehicle of abstract enthusiasm,
The world's dynamic void!

Let's leave Being behind us.
Let's leave for good this small town called Life,
This suburb-World of God,
And let's venture into the city headlong,
Without stopping, just madly Going . . .
Let's set off once and for all.

When does the last train leave for where you are, Walt?
What God was I that my nostalgia should arouse such
    yearnings?
Perhaps by departing I'll return. Perhaps by ending I'll
    arrive—
Who knows? Any time is the right time. Let's leave,
Come on! We've tarried too long. To leave is to have
    already gone.

Let's leave for where everything stays put.
O road to no-more-roads!
The last stop of No-Stopping!

◆

In my poems I sing of trains, automobiles, and steamers,
But however high I hoist my poem, it has only rhythms
    and ideas,
It has no steel, iron or wheels, it has no wood, no ropes,
It lacks the reality of a road's most negligible stone,
The stone people step on without ever looking at it
But which may be looked at, picked up, stepped on.
Whereas my poems are sounds and ideas that might not be
    understood.

What I want is iron, not just to sing of iron.
What I think gives only the idea of steel, not the steel.
What infuriates me in all my mind's emotions
Is that I can't swap my rhythm that mimics rippling water
For the real coolness of water on my hands,
For the visible sound of the river where I can enter and
    get wet,
Which can drench my suit,
Where I can drown myself, if I like,
And which has the natural divinity of existing without
    literature.
Shit! A thousand times shit for everything I can't do.
But what, Walt (can you hear me?), is everything, everything,
    everything?

Damn the tragedy of our not being God
Such that our flesh could write poems in Universes and
    Realities,
And our ideas be things, our thoughts Infinity!
And I'd have real stars in my thinking-being,
Number-names in every corner of my emotion-Earth.

◆

The true modern poem is life without poems,
It's the train itself and not the verses that sing of it,

It's the iron of the rails, the hot rails, the iron of the wheels,
    their actual spin,
And not my poems that talk about rails and wheels without
    iron or spin.

◆

The wind-up or string-pulled train of a child
Has more real motion than our poems . . .
Our poems that don't have wheels,
Our poems that go nowhere,
Our unread poems that never leave the page.
(I'm sick of life, sick of art,
Sick of not having things, either out of lack or out of fear—
My breathing like a practical joke to torment me,
My self-image like a ridiculous carnival puppet.
When does the last train leave?)

I know that singing in this way isn't to sing of you,
    but so what?
I know it's to sing of everything, but to sing of
    everything is to sing of you.
I know it's to sing of myself, but to sing of myself is to sing
    of you.
I know that even to say I can't sing is to sing of you, Walt . . .

◆

To sing of you,
To salute you,
I'd have to write the supreme poem
Which, more than any other supreme poem, would embrace
In a total synthesis (based on an exhaustive analysis)
The whole Universe of things, living beings and souls,
The whole Universe of men, women and children,
The whole Universe of acts, gestures, feelings, thoughts,
The whole Universe of the things humanity makes
And the things humanity experiences—
Professions, laws, norms, medical sciences, Fate,
Written this way and that, constantly crisscrossing
On the dynamic paper of Events,

On the quick papyrus of social groupings,
On the palimpsest of continuously renewed emotions.

◆

For me to salute you,
To salute you as you should be saluted,
I need to make my verses into a steed,
Make my verses into a train,
Make my verses into an arrow,
Make my verses sheer speed,
Make my verses the things of the world.

You sang everything, and in you everything sang—
Magnificent whorish receptivity
Of your sensations with their legs wide open
To the outlines and details of the whole universe.

◆

Hup-hup what, or why, or to where?
Hup-hup to what end?
Hup-hup to where, make-believe steed?
Hup-hup to where, imaginary train?
Hup-hup to where, O arrow, haste and speed
Which are all just me pining after you,
All just me feeling your absence in every last nerve?

Hup-hup to where, if there is no where or how?
Hup-hup to where, if I'm always where I am and
    never up ahead,
Never ahead and never behind
But always irremediably in the place of my body,
All too humanly in the thinking center of my soul,
Always the same indivisible atom of the divine personality?

Hup-hup to where, O sadness of not achieving what I want?
Hup-hup to where and for what? Hup-hup what or without
    what?
Hup-hup-hup, but where to, O my uncertainty?

If only I could stop writing verse on verse on verse about iron
And see, have and be iron instead, and have that be my
    poetry,
Poetry-iron-poetry, psycho-physio-I circle!

(When does the last train leave?)

◆

Time for our vitality to declare bankruptcy!
We write poetry, singing of things we fail to live.
If only there were a way to live all lives and all ages
And all forms of form
And all gestures of gestures!
What's the writing of poetry but a confession that life isn't
    enough?
What's art but a way to forget that life is just this?

Farewell, Walt, farewell!
Farewell until the indefinite that lies beyond the End.
Wait for me, if where you are you can wait.
When does the last train leave?
When do we leave?

◆

Hup-hup? Hup what and hup why?
What do I get from *hup-hup* or from anything
Prompting me to think of *hup-hup*?

Decadents, old boy, that's what we are . . .
Deep down in each of us there's a Byzantium in flames,
And although I don't feel the flames and don't feel
    Byzantium,
The Empire is dying out in our watery veins,
And Poetry was but our incapacity to act . . .
You, singer of vigorous professions, You the Poet of the
    Strong and the Extreme,
You, inspiration's muscle, ruled by male muses,
You, finally, an innocent in a state of hysteria,

Finally just a "caresser of life,"
A shiftless idler, a pansy at least in spirit.
That was your business, nobody else's, but where's Life
    in all that?

I, an engineer by profession, sick of everything and everyone,
I, absolutely superfluous, at war with things,
I, useless, worn-out, unproductive, pretentious and amoral,
Buoy of my sensations scattered by the storm,
Anchor in the depths that broke off from my ship,
I—can you believe it?—a singer of Life and Power,
I, healthy and vigorous like you in my poems,
And even sincere like you, burning with all Europe
    in my brain,
In my explosive brain with no dikes to contain it,
In my dynamic master intelligence,
In my trademark, projector, bank-check, rubber-stamp
    sensuality.
Why the devil do we live, and write verses?
Damn the sloth that makes us poets,
The degeneracy that fools us into thinking we're artists,
The fundamental tedium that tries to pass us off as energetic
    and modern
When all we really want is to amuse ourselves, to savor an
    idea of life,
Since we do nothing and are nothing, life limply flowing
    through our veins.

Let's at least see things as they really are, Walt . . .
Let's swallow all this like a bitter pill
And agree to send life and the world to hell
Because we're tired of looking at it, not because we abhor or
    disdain it.

Is this any way to salute you?
Whatever it is, it's to salute you.
Whatever it's worth, it's to love you.
Whatever it comes to, it's to agree with you.

Whatever it is, it's this. And you understand, you like it.
You, old boy, crying on my shoulder, agree with me . . .
(When does the last train leave?
A long holiday spent in God . . .
Let's go without fear, let's go . . .)
All this must have another meaning
Beyond just living and having all we have . . .
There must be a point of consciousness
In which the landscape is transformed
And begins to interest us, arouse us, shake us up,
In which a cool breeze stirs in our soul
And sunny fields open up in our lately awakened
      senses . . .
We'll meet at the Station, wherever it is . . .
Wait for me at the entrance, Walt; I'll be there . . .
I'll be there without the universe, without life, without
      myself, without anything . . .
And together we'll remember, in the silence of our own idea,
The world's tremendous absurdity, the bitter inadequacy of
      things,
And I'll feel the great mystery, I'll feel it far away, so far
      away,
So abstractly and absolutely far away,
Definitively far away.

◆

I stop, I listen, I recognize myself!
The sound of my voice in the air has fallen, lifeless.
I'm the same as I was, you are dead, and everything is
      still . . .
Saluting you was a way of trying to inject life into myself,
And so I saluted you in spite of feeling that I lack
The vital energy to salute anyone!

O heart that won't heal! Who will save me from you?

[1915]

All along the wharf there's the bustle of an imminent arrival.
People begin to gather around and wait.
The steamer from Africa is coming into plain view.
I came here to wait for no one,
To watch everyone else wait,
To be everyone else waiting,
To be the anxious waiting of everyone else.

I'm exhausted from being so many things.
The latecomers are finally arriving,
And I suddenly get sick of waiting, of existing, of being.
I abruptly leave and am noticed by the gatekeeper, who
    gives me a hard, quick stare.
I return to the city as if to freedom.

It's good to feel, if for no other reason, so as to stop feeling.

LISBON REVISITED (1923)

No, I don't want anything.
I already said I don't want anything.

Don't come to me with conclusions!
Death is the only conclusion.

Don't offer me aesthetics!
Don't talk to me of morals!
Take metaphysics away from here!
Don't try to sell me complete systems, don't bore me
    with the breakthroughs
Of science (of science, my God, of science!)—
Of science, of the arts, of modern civilization!

What harm did I ever do to the gods?

If you've got the truth, you can keep it!

I'm a technician, but my technique is limited to the technical
    sphere,
Apart from which I'm crazy, and with every right to be so.
With every right to be so, do you hear?

Leave me alone, for God's sake!

You want me to be married, futile, conventional and taxable?
You want me to be the opposite of this, the opposite of
    anything?

If I were someone else, I'd go along with you all.
But since I'm what I am, lay off!
Go to hell without me,
Or let me go there by myself!
Why do we have to go together?

Don't grab me by the arm!
I don't like my arm being grabbed. I want to be alone.
I already told you that I can only be alone!
I'm sick of you wanting me to be sociable!

O blue sky—the same one I knew as a child—
Perfect and empty eternal truth!
O gentle, silent, ancestral Tagus,
Tiny truth in which the sky is mirrored!
O sorrow revisited, Lisbon of bygone days today!
You give me nothing, you take nothing from me, you're
    nothing I feel is me.

Leave me in peace! I won't stay long, for I never stay
    long . . .
And as long as Silence and the Abyss hold off, I want to be
    alone!

[1923]

LISBON REVISITED (1926)

Nothing holds me.
I want fifty things at the same time.
I long with meat-craving anxiety
For I don't know what—
Definitely something indefinite . . .
I sleep fitfully and live in the fitful dream-state
Of a fitful sleeper, half dreaming.

All abstract and necessary doors were closed in my face.
Curtains were drawn across every hypothesis I could see
    from the street.
I found the alley but not the number of the address I was
    given.

I woke up to the same life I'd fallen asleep to.
Even the armies I dreamed of were defeated.
Even my dreams felt false while I dreamed them.
Even the life I merely long for jades me—even that life . . .

At intermittent intervals I understand;
I write in respites from my weariness;
And a boredom bored even of itself casts me ashore.

I don't know what destiny or future belongs to my anxiety
    adrift on the waves;
I don't know what impossible South Sea islands await me, a
    castaway,

Or what palm groves of literature will grant me at least a
　　line of verse.

No, I don't know this, or that, or anything else . . .
And in the depths of my spirit, where I dream all I've
　　dreamed,
In my soul's far-flung fields, where I remember for no reason
(And the past is a natural mist of false tears),
On the roads and pathways of distant forests
Where I supposed my being dwelled—
There my dreamed armies, defeated without having been,
And my nonexistent legions, annihilated in God,
All flee in disarray, the last remnants
Of the final illusion.

Once more I see you,
City of my horrifyingly lost childhood . . .
Happy and sad city, once more I dream here . . .
I? Is it one and the same I who lived here, and came back,
And came back again, and again,
And yet again have come back?
Or are we—all the I's that I was here or that were here—
A series of bead-beings joined together by a string of
　　memory,
A series of dreams about me dreamed by someone outside
　　me?

Once more I see you,
With a heart that's more distant, a soul that's less mine.

Once more I see you—Lisbon, the Tagus, and the rest—
A useless onlooker of you and of myself,
A foreigner here like everywhere else,
Incidental in life as in my soul,
A ghost wandering through halls of remembrances
To the sound of rats and creaking floorboards
In the accursed castle of having to live . . .

Once more I see you,
A shadow moving among shadows, gleaming
For an instant in some bleak unknown light
Before passing into the night like a ship's wake swallowed
In water whose sound fades into silence . . .

Once more I see you,
But, oh, I cannot see myself!
The magic mirror where I always looked the same has
    shattered,
And in each fateful fragment I see only a piece of me—
A piece of you and of me!

26 APRIL 1926

If you want to kill yourself, why don't you want to kill
    yourself?
Now's your chance! I, who greatly love both death and life,
Would kill myself too, if I dared kill myself . . .
If you dare, then be daring!
What good to you is the changing picture of outer images
We call the world?
What good is this cinema of hours played out
By actors with stock roles and gestures,
This colorful circus of our never-ending drive to keep going?
What good is your inner world which you don't know?
Kill yourself, and maybe you'll finally know it . . .
End it all, and maybe you'll begin . . .
If you're weary of existing, at least
Be noble in your weariness,
And don't, like me, sing of life because you're drunk,
Don't, like me, salute death through literature!

You're needed? O futile shadow called man!
No one is needed; you're not needed by anyone . . .
Without you everything will keep going without you.
Perhaps it's worse for others that you live than if you kill
    yourself . . .
Perhaps your presence is more burdensome than your
    absence . . .

Other people's grief? You're worried
About them crying over you?

Don't worry: they won't cry for long . . .
The impulse to live gradually stanches tears
When they're not for our own sake,
When they're because of what happened to someone else,
    especially death,
Since after this happens to someone, nothing else will . . .

First there's anguish, the surprise of mystery's arrival
And of your spoken life's sudden absence . . .
Then there's the horror of your visible and material coffin,
And the men in black whose profession is to be there.
Then the attending family, heartbroken and telling jokes,
Mourning between the latest news from the evening papers,
Mingling grief over your death with the latest crime . . .
And you merely the incidental cause of that lamentation,
You who will be truly dead, much deader than you
    imagine . . .
Much deader down here than you imagine,
Even if in the beyond you may be much more alive . . .

Next comes the black procession to the vault or grave,
And finally the beginning of the death of your memory.
At first everyone feels relieved
That the slightly irksome tragedy of your death is over . . .
Then, with each passing day, the conversation lightens up
And life falls back into its old routine . . .

Then you are slowly forgotten.
You're remembered only twice a year:
On your birthday and your death day.
That's it. That's all. That's absolutely all.
Two times a year they think about you.
Two times a year those who loved you heave a sigh,
And they may sigh on the rare occasions someone mentions
    your name.

Look honestly at yourself and into what we are . . .
If you want to kill yourself, then kill yourself . . .

Forget your moral scruples or intellectual qualms!
What scruples or qualms influence the workings of life?
What chemical scruples rule the driving impulse
Of sap, the blood's circulation, and love?
What memory of others exists in the joyous rhythm of life?

Oh, vanity of flesh and blood called man,
Can't you see that you're utterly unimportant?

You're important to yourself, because you're what you feel.
You're everything to yourself, because for you you're the
    universe,
While the real universe and other people
Are mere satellites of your objective subjectivity.
You matter to yourself, because you're all that matters to
    you.
And if this is true for you, O myth, then won't it be true for
    others?

Do you, like Hamlet, dread the unknown?
But what is known? What do you really know
Such that you can call anything "unknown"?

Do you, like Falstaff, love life with all its fat?
If you love it so materially, then love it even more materially
By becoming a bodily part of the earth and of things!
Scatter yourself, O physicochemical system
Of nocturnally conscious cells,
Over the nocturnal consciousness of the unconsciousness of
    bodies,
Over the huge blanket of appearances that blankets nothing,
Over the grass and weeds of proliferating beings,
Over the atomic fog of things,
Over the whirling walls
Of the dynamic void that's the world . . .

26 APRIL 1926

Distant lighthouses
With their light suddenly so bright,
With night and absence so swiftly restored,
On this night, on this deck—the anguish they stir up!
The last of our grieving for those we left behind,
Fiction of thinking . . .

Distant lighthouses . . .
Life's uncertainty . . .
The fast-swelling light has returned, flashing
In the aimlessness of my lost gaze.

Distant lighthouses . . .
Life serves no purpose.
Thinking about life serves no purpose.
Thinking about thinking about life serves no purpose.

We're going far away and the bright light begins to flash less
    brightly.
Distant lighthouses . . .

                                        30 APRIL 1926

SQUIB

All the Lloyd Georges of Babylon
Were utterly forgotten by history.
The Briands of Egypt or Assyria,
The Trotskys of this or that colony
Of ancient Greece or Rome
Are dead names, though writ in stone.

Only a fool who makes poems
Or a mad inventor of philosophies
Or an eccentric geometrician
Will survive the vast unimportance
Of what's left behind, in the dark,
And which not even history remarks.

O you great men of the Moment!
O great and ardent glories
Of those who flee obscurity!
Enjoy what you have and don't think!
Cherish your fame and good food,
For tomorrow belongs to today's fools!

[1926]

At the wheel of the Chevrolet on the road to Sintra,
In the moonlight and in a dream, on the deserted road,
I drive alone, I drive almost slowly, and it almost
Seems, or I make myself think it seems,
That I'm going down another road, another dream, another
    world,
That I'm going without Lisbon lying behind me and Sintra
    up ahead,
That I'm going, and what's in it besides not stopping, just
    going?

I'll spend the night in Sintra since I can't spend it in Lisbon,
But when I get to Sintra I'll be sorry I didn't stay in Lisbon.
Always this irrational, irrelevant, useless fretfulness,
Always, always, always
This exaggerated mental anxiety over nothing,
On the road to Sintra, on the road of dreaming, on the road
    of life . . .

Responsive to my subconscious movements at the wheel,
The borrowed car bounds forward beneath me, with me.
As I think about the symbol and turn right, I smile.
How many borrowed things I've used to go forward in the
    world!
How many borrowed things I've driven as if they
    were mine!
Alas, how much I myself am what I've borrowed!

On the left side of the road there's the hovel of a house—yes,
    a hovel.
On the right the open country, with the moon in the
    distance.
The car, which so recently seemed to be giving me freedom,
Is now something that encloses me,
Something I can only drive if I'm closed up inside it,
Something I control only if I'm part of it, if it's part of me.

Behind me on the left is the humble—more than humble—
    house . . .
Life there must be happy, just because it isn't mine.
If anyone saw me from the window, they're no doubt
    thinking: *That* guy is happy.
Perhaps to the child peering out the top-floor window
I looked (with my borrowed car) like a dream, a magical
    being come to life.
Perhaps to the girl, who as soon as she heard the motor
    looked out the kitchen window
On the ground floor,
I'm something like the prince of every girl's heart,
And she'll keep glancing through the window until I vanish
    around the curve.
Will I leave dreams behind me, or is it the car that leaves them?
I the driver of the borrowed car, or the borrowed car I'm
    driving?

On the road to Sintra in the moonlight, in sadness, with
    fields and the night before me,
Driving the borrowed Chevrolet and feeling forlorn,
I lose myself on the road to come, I vanish in the distance I'm
    covering,
And on a sudden, frantic, violent, inexplicable impulse
I accelerate . . .
But my heart is still back at that heap of stones I skirted
    when I saw it without seeing it,
At the door of the hovel,
My empty heart,

My dissatisfied heart,
My heart that's more human than I, more exact than life.

On the road to Sintra, close to midnight, in the moonlight,
    at the wheel,
On the road to Sintra, exhausted just from imagining,
On the road to Sintra, ever closer to Sintra,
On the road to Sintra, ever farther from myself . . .

11 MAY 1928

CLOUDS

On this sad day my heart sadder than the day . . .
Moral and civic obligations?
The intricate web of duties, of consequences?
No, nothing . . .
A sad day, an apathy toward everything . . .
Nothing . . .

Others travel (I've also traveled), others are out in the sun
(I've also been out in the sun, or imagined I was),
Others have purpose, or life, or symmetrical ignorance,
Vanity, happiness, and sociability,
And they immigrate to return one day, or not to return,
On ships that simply transport them.
They don't feel the death that lurks in every departure,
The mystery behind every arrival,
The horror within everything new . . .
They don't feel: that's why they're legislators and
      financiers,
Go dancing and work as office employees,
Go to shows and meet people . . .
They don't feel—why should they?

Let these clothed cattle from the stables of the Gods
Go on by, decked with garlands for the sacrifice,
Warmed by the sun, cheerful, lively, and content to be so . . .
Let them go, but alas, I'm going with them without a garland
To the same destination!

I'm going with them without the sun I can feel, without the
   life I have,
I'm going with them without ignorance . . .

On this sad day my heart sadder than the day . . .
On this sad day every day . . .
On this very sad day . . .

13 MAY 1928

ENGLISH SONG

I broke with the sun and stars. I let the world go.
I went far and wide with the knapsack of things I know.
I made the journey, bought the useless, found the indefinite,
And my heart is the same as it was: a sky and a desert.
I failed in what I was, in what I wanted, in what I
    discovered.
I've no soul left for light to arouse or darkness to smother.
I'm nothing but nausea, nothing but reverie, nothing but
    longing.
I'm something very far removed, and I keep going
Just because my I feels cozy and profoundly real,
Stuck like a wad of spit to one of the world's wheels.

1 DECEMBER 1928

CHANCE

In the street where all is chance the blonde girl chances by.
But no, it's a different one.

The other girl was on another street, in another city, and I
    was another.

I suddenly stray from the sight in front of me,
I'm back in the other city, on the other street,
And the other girl walks by.

What an advantage to have an intransigent memory!
Now I regret never again having seen the other girl,
And I regret not even having looked at this one.

What an advantage to have a soul turned inside out!
At least some verses get written.
Verses get written, one passes for a madman, and then a
    genius
If luck will have it, or even if it won't—
The marvel of celebrity!

I was saying that at least some verses get written . . .
This was with respect to a girl,
A blonde girl,
But which one?
There was one I saw a long time ago in another city,
On another sort of street,
And there's this one I saw a long time ago in another city,

On another sort of street.
Since all memories are the same memory,
Everything that was is the same death,
Yesterday, today, and maybe even tomorrow.

A passerby looks at me with casual curiosity.
Could it be that I'm making verses in gestures and frowns?
Perhaps . . . The blonde girl?
It's the same girl after all . . .
Everything's the same after all . . .

Only I am in some sense not the same, and this is also the
    same.

27 MARCH 1929

NOTE

My soul shattered like an empty vase.
It fell irretrievably down the stairs.
If fell from the hands of the careless maid.
It fell, breaking into more pieces than there was china in
the vase.

Nonsense? Impossible? I'm not so sure!
I have more sensations than when I felt like myself.
I'm a heap of shards on a doormat that needs shaking.

My fall made a noise like a shattering vase.
Whatever gods there are lean over the stair rail
And look at the shards their maid changed me into.

They don't get mad at her.
They're forgiving.
What was I but an empty vase?

They look at the absurdly conscious shards—
Conscious of themselves, not of the gods.

They look and smile.
They smile forgivingly at the unwitting maid.

The great staircase carpeted with stars stretches across
the sky.
A shard gleams, shiny side up, among the heavenly bodies.

My work? My primary soul? My life?
A shard.
And the gods stare at it, intrigued, not knowing why it's
    there.

ALMOST

To put my life in order, with shelves for my will and my
  action . . .
That's what I want to do, as I've always wanted, with the
  same result.
But how good it is to have the clear intention—firm only in
  its clearness—of doing something!

I'm going to pack my suitcases for the Definitive,
I'm going to organize Álvaro de Campos,
And be at the same point tomorrow as the day before
  yesterday—a day before yesterday that's always . . .

I smile in anticipation of the nothing I'll be.
At least I smile: to smile is something.

We're all products of Romanticism,
And if we weren't products of Romanticism, we probably
  wouldn't be anything.

That's how literature happens . . .
And it's also (sorry, Gods!) how life happens.

Everyone else is also a Romantic,
Everyone else also achieves nothing and is either rich or
  poor,
Everyone else also spends life looking at suitcases that still
  need to be packed,

Everyone else also falls asleep next to a clutter of papers,
Everyone else is also me.

Peddler crying out her wares like an unconscious hymn,
Tiny cogwheel in the clockwork of political economy,
Present or future mother of those who die when Empires
    crumble,
Your voice reaches me like a summons to nowhere, like the
    silence of life . . .

I look up from the papers I'm thinking of not putting in order
    after all
To the window through which I didn't see—I just heard—the
    peddler,
And my smile, which still hadn't ended, ends in metaphysics
    inside my brain.

I disbelieved in all the gods while sitting at a cluttered desk,
I looked all destinies in the face because I was distracted by
    a shouting peddler,
My weariness is an old boat rotting on a deserted beach,
And with this image from some other poet I close my desk
    and the poem.

Like a god, I've put neither truth nor life in order.

15 MAY 1929

I have a bad cold,
And everyone knows how bad colds
Throw the whole universe out of kilter.
They turn us against life
And make us sneeze even metaphysically.
I've wasted the whole day blowing my nose.
My head hurts all over.
A sorry state for a minor poet!
Today I'm truly a minor poet.
What I used to be was a wish: it snapped.

Goodbye forever, Fairy Queen!
You had wings of sunlight, and here I am plodding along.
I won't get well unless I lie down in bed.
I've never been well except when lying down in the universe.
Excusez du peu . . . What a terrible physical cold!
I need truth and some aspirin.

14 MARCH 1931

OXFORDSHIRE

I want the good, I want the bad, and in the end I want
    nothing.
I toss in bed, uncomfortable on my right side, on my left
    side,
And on my consciousness of existing.
I'm universally uncomfortable, metaphysically
    uncomfortable,
But what's even worse is my headache.
That's more serious than the meaning of the universe.

Once, while walking in the country around Oxford,
I saw up ahead, beyond a bend in the road,
A church steeple towering above the houses of a hamlet or
    village.
The photographic image of that nonevent has remained
    with me
Like a horizontal wrinkle marring a trouser's crease.
Today it seems relevant . . .
From the road I associated that steeple with spirituality,
The faith of all ages, and practical charity.
When I arrived at the village, the steeple was a steeple
And, what's more, there it was.

You can be happy in Australia, as long as you don't go there.

4 JUNE 1931

Yes it's me, I myself, what I turned out to be,
A kind of accessory or spare part of my own person,
The jagged outskirts of my true emotion—
I'm the one here in myself, it's me.

Whatever I was, whatever I wasn't—it's all in what I am.
Whatever I wanted, whatever I didn't want—all of this has
    shaped me.
Whatever I loved, or stopped loving—in me it's the same
    nostalgia.

And I also have the impression—a bit inconsistent,
Like a dream based on jumbled realities—
That I left myself on a seat in the streetcar,
To be found by whoever was going to sit down there next.

And I also have the impression—a bit hazy,
Like a dream one tries to remember on waking up to the dim
    light of dawn—
That there's something better in me than myself.

Yes, I also have the impression—a bit painful,
As of waking up without dreams to a day full of creditors—
That I bungled everything, like tripping on a doormat,
That I got everything wrong, like a suitcase without toilet
    articles,
That I replaced myself with something at some point in my
    life.

Enough! It's the impression—somewhat metaphysical,
Like the last sun seen in the window of a house we're about
    to abandon—
That it's better to be a child than to want to fathom the
    world.
It's the impression of buttered bread and toys,
Of a vast peace without any gardens of Proserpine,
Of an enthusiasm for life, its face pressed against the
    window,
Seeing the rain pattering outside
Rather than the adult tears from having a knot in our throat.

Enough, damn it, enough! It's me, the one who got switched,
The emissary with no letter or credentials,
The clown who doesn't laugh, the jester wearing someone
    else's oversize suit,
And the bells on his hat jingle
Like little cowbells of a servitude weighing on his head.

It's me, I myself, the singsong riddle
That no one can figure out in the rural sitting room after
    dinner.

It's me, just me, and nothing I can do about it!

6 AUGUST 1931

AH, A SONNET . . .

My heart is a mad admiral
Who quit his life at sea
And remembers it little by little
At home, pacing, pacing . . .

With this motion (the mere thought
Of which makes me shift in my seat)
The seas he once sailed still toss
In his muscles bored of inactivity.

Nostalgia's in his legs and arms.
Nostalgia pours out of his brain.
His boredom turns into raving.

But if, for God's sake, the heart
Was my theme, why is this poem dealing
With an admiral instead of with feeling?

12 OCTOBER 1931

My heart, the deluded admiral
Who ruled a fleet of never-built ships,
Followed a route Fate wouldn't admit,
In search of an impossible happiness.

Absurd, verbose, always on the shelf,
Given to a life that merely abstains,
He never gave himself, gave himself, gave himself,
As the run-on verse explains.

But there are advantages to a history
Lived in the shadows; the silence of defeat
Has inner roses unknown to victory.

And so the admiral's imperial fleet,
Laden with yearnings and dreams of glory,
Followed its course with no retreat.

Speak softly, for this is life,
Life and my consciousness of it,
Because the night advances, I'm tired, I can't sleep,
And if I go to the window
I see, beneath my brutish eyelids, the stars' many
    dwellings . . .
I wore out the day hoping I'd sleep at night.
Now it's night, almost the next day. I'm sleepy. I can't sleep.
I feel, in this weariness, that I'm all of humanity.
It's a weariness that almost turns my bones into foam . . .
We all share the same lot . . .
Flies with caught wings, we stagger
Through the world, a spider web spanning the abyss.

21 OCTOBER 1931

I wake up in the middle of the night and its silence.
I see—ticktock—that it's four hours until morning.
In the despair of my insomnia I throw open the window.
And across the way I see the human,
Crisscrossed rectangle of another lit window!
Fraternity in the night!

Involuntary, secret fraternity in the night!
We're both awake, and humanity doesn't know.
It sleeps. We have light.

Who are you? A sick man, a counterfeiter, or just an
    insomniac like me?
It doesn't matter. The eternal, formless, infinite night
Has only, in this place, the humanity of our two windows,
The quiet heart of our two lights.
In this place and time, strangers to each other, we're all of life.
At the window in the back room of my apartment,
Feeling the damp of night on the wooden sill,
I lean out toward the infinite, and a bit toward myself.

Not even a rooster disturbs the still definitive silence!
What are you doing, comrade of that lit window?
Am I, in my insomnia, dreaming life?
Round yellow glow of your secret window . . .
Funny: you don't have electric light.
O kerosene lamps of my lost childhood!

25 NOVEMBER 1931

MAGNIFICAT

When will this inner night—the universe—end
And I—my soul—have my day?
When will I wake up from being awake?
I don't know. The sun shines on high
And cannot be looked at.
The stars coldly blink
And cannot be counted.
The heart beats aloofly
And cannot be heard.
When will this drama without theater
—Or this theater without drama—end
So that I can go home?
Where? How? When?
O cat staring at me with eyes of life, Who lurks in your
  depths?
It's Him! It's him!
Like Joshua he'll order the sun to stop, and I'll wake up,
And it will be day.
Smile, my soul, in your slumber!
Smile, my soul: it will be day!

7 NOVEMBER 1933

ORIGINAL SIN

Who will write the history of what could have been?
That, if someone writes it,
Will be the true history of humanity.

What exists is the real world—not us, just the world.
We are, in reality, what doesn't exist.

I am who I failed to be.
We are all who we supposed ourselves.
Our reality is what we never attained.

What happened to that truth we had—the dream at the
    window of childhood?
What happened to our certainty—the plans at the desk that
    followed?

Sitting sideways in a chair after dinner, with my head
Resting against my folded hands, which are resting
Against the high sill of the balcony window, I ponder.

What happened to my reality, that all I have is life?
What happened to me, that I'm just who I am?

How many Caesars I've been!

In my soul, and with some truth;
In my imagination, and with some justice;

In my intellect, and with some warrant—
My God! My God! My God!—
How many Caesars I've been!
How many Caesars I've been!
How many Caesars I've been!

THE WORLD, 7 DECEMBER 1933

Lisbon with its houses
Of various colors,
Lisbon with its houses
Of various colors,
Lisbon with its houses
Of various colors . . .
By virtue of being different, this is monotonous,
Just as, by virtue of feeling, I do nothing but
    think.

At night, lying down but awake
In the useless lucidity of not being able to sleep,
I try to imagine something
But something else always appears (since I'm
    sleepy
And, being sleepy, a bit dreamy).
I try to extend the range of my imagination
To fantastic, sprawling palm groves,
But all I see
On what seems to be the inside of my eyelids
Is Lisbon with its houses
Of various colors.

I smile because here, lying down, it's something else.
By virtue of being monotonous, it's different.
And, by virtue of being I, I fall asleep and forget
    I exist.

What remains, without me, whom I've forgotten since I'm
    asleep,
Is Lisbon with its houses
Of various colors.

11 MAY 1934

What happiness there is
In the building across the street from me and my dreams!

It's inhabited by people I don't know, whom I've seen but
    not seen.
They're happy, because they're not me.

The children who play on the high balconies
Live forever, without doubt,
Among flowerpots.

The voices rising from inside the homes
Always sing, without doubt.
Yes, they must sing.

When there's feasting out here, there's feasting in there,
Which is bound to be the case where everything's in
    agreement:
People with Nature, because the city is Nature.

What tremendous happiness not to be me!

But don't others feel the same way?
What others? There are no others.
What others feel is a home with shut windows,
And when they're opened
It's for their children to play on the railed balcony,
Among the pots with I don't know what sort of flowers.

Other people never feel.
We're the ones who feel,
Yes, all of us,
Even I, who am feeling nothing right now.

Nothing? Well . . .
A slight pain that's nothing . . .

16 JUNE 1934

I got off the train
And said goodbye to the man I'd met.
We'd been together for eighteen hours
And had a pleasant conversation,
Fellowship in the journey,
And I was sorry to get off, sorry to leave
This chance friend whose name I never learned.
I felt my eyes water with tears . . .
Every farewell is a death.
Yes, every farewell is a death.
In the train that we call life
We are all chance events in one another's lives,
And we all feel sorry when it's time to get off.

All that is human moves me, because I'm a man.
All that is human moves me not because I have an affinity
With human ideas or human doctrines
But because of my infinite fellowship with humanity itself.

The maid who hated to go,
Crying with nostalgia
For the house where she'd been mistreated . . .

All of this, inside my heart, is death and the sadness of leaving.
All of this lives, because it dies, inside my heart.

And my heart is a little larger than the entire universe.

4 JULY 1934

How long it's been since I could write
A long poem!
It's been years . . .

I've lost that capacity for rhythmic development
In which idea and form
Move forward together
In a unity of body and soul . . .

I've lost everything that once gave me
Some sense of an inner certainty . . .
What do I have left?
The sun, which is there without me having summoned it . . .
The day, which requires no effort on my part . . .
A breeze, or the lack of a breeze,
Making me conscious of the air . . .
And the domestic egoism of wanting nothing else.

But oh, my "Triumphal Ode,"
With its rectilinear movement!
Oh, my "Maritime Ode,"
With its development in strophe, antistrophe and epode!
And my plans, all my plans,
Which were my greatest odes of all!
And that final, supreme, impossible ode!

9 AUGUST 1934

The stillness of midnight begins to descend
On the various floors of accumulated life
Which make up this apartment building.
The piano on the third floor has quieted.
I hear no more steps on the second.
On the ground floor the radio is silent.

Everything's going to sleep . . .

I'm alone with the entire universe.
I don't even feel like going to the window.
If I looked out, what stars I'd see!
How much vaster are the lofty silences!
How anti-urban is the sky!

Instead, secluded in my desire
Not to be secluded,
I anxiously listen to the sounds from the street.
An automobile—zoom!—perks me up . . .
Doubled steps in conversation speak to me . . .
The clank of a brusquely shut gate pains me . . .

Everything's going to sleep . . .

Only I remain awake, drowsily listening,
Waiting
For something before going to sleep.
Something . . .

9 AUGUST 1934

I took off the mask and looked in the mirror.
I was the same child I was years ago.
I hadn't changed at all . . .

That's the advantage of knowing how to remove your mask.
You're still the child,
The past that lives on,
The child.

I took off the mask, and I put it back on.
It's better this way.
This way I'm the mask.

And I return to normality as to a streetcar terminus.

11 AUGUST 1934

I, I myself . . .
I, full of all the weariness
The world can produce . . .
I . . .

Everything, finally, since everything is me,
Including even the stars, it seems,
Came out of my pocket to dazzle children.
What children I don't know . . .
I . . .

Imperfect? Inscrutable? Divine?
I don't know.
I . . .

Did I have a past? Of course.
Do I have a present? Of course.
Will I have a future? Of course,
Even if it doesn't last long.
But I, I . . .
I am I,
I remain I,
I . . .

4 JANUARY 1935

HOMECOMING

It's been years since my last sonnet,
But I'll try to write one anyhow.
Sonnets belong to childhood, and now
My childhood is just a black dot,

Which throws me off the forever unmoving
Ongoing journey of the train that's me.
And the sonnet's like someone inhabiting
(For two days now) my mind's constant musing.

Thank God I still remember that
It takes fourteen lines of equal length,
So people will know where they're at . . .

But where people are, or where I am,
I don't know and couldn't care less,
And whatever I do know can be damned.

3 FEBRUARY 1935

Yes, everything's just fine.
It's all perfectly fine.
Except for one thing: it's all screwed up.
I know my building is painted gray,
I know what the number of the building is,
I don't know but can find out its assessed value
In the tax offices that exist for that purpose.
I know, I know . . .
But I also know there are people who live here,
And the Public Revenue Office couldn't exempt
My next-door neighbor from the death of her son.
And the Bureau of What-Have-You couldn't prevent
The husband of the lady upstairs from running off with her
    sister.
But everything, of course, is just fine . . .
And except for the fact it's all screwed up, it really is just fine.

5 MARCH 1935

I'm dizzy.
Dizzy from too much sleeping or too much thinking
Or too much of both.
All I know is I'm dizzy,
And I'm not sure if I should get up from my chair
Or how I would get up from it.
I'm dizzy—let's leave it at that.

What life
Did I make out of life?
None.
It all happened in the cracks,
It was all approximations,
All a function of the abnormal and the absurd,
All essentially nothing . . .
That's why I'm dizzy.

Now
Every morning I wake up
Dizzy . . .
Yes, literally dizzy . . .
Unsure of my own name,
Unsure of where I am,
Unsure of what I've been,
Unsure of everything.

But if that's how it is, that's how it is.
So I remain in the chair.

I'm dizzy.
That's right, I'm dizzy.
I remain seated
And dizzy.
Yes, dizzy.
Dizzy . . .
Dizzy . . .

12 SEPTEMBER 1935

POEM IN A STRAIGHT LINE

I've never known anyone who took a beating.
All my acquaintances have been champions at everything.

Whereas I, so often shabby, so often disgusting, so often
    despicable,
I, so often and undeniably a sponger,
Inexcusably filthy,
I, who so often have been too lazy to take a bath,
I, who so often have been ridiculous and absurd,
Who have tripped in public on the rugs of etiquette,
Who have been grotesque, petty, obsequious and arrogant,
Who have been humiliated and said nothing,
Who, when I've spoken up, have been even more ridiculous,
I, who have been the laughingstock of chambermaids,
Who have felt errand boys winking behind my back,
Who have been a financial disgrace, borrowing money I never
    paid back,
Who, when punches were about to fly, ducked
Out of punching range—
I, who have anguished over the pettiest things,
Am convinced there's no one in the world as pathetic as me.

No one I know has ever done anything ridiculous.
No one who talks to me has ever been humiliated.
They've been princes in life, every last one of them . . .

If only I could hear some other human voice
Confess not to a sin but to an infamy,

Tell not about an act of violence but of cowardice!
No, all the people I listen to, if they talk to me, are paragons.
Who in this wide world would admit to me that they were
    ever despicable?
O princes, my brothers,

I've had it up to here with demigods!
Where in the world are there people?

Am I the only one on earth who's ever wrong and despicable?

They may not have been loved by women,
They may have been cheated on—but ridiculous, never!
And I, who have been ridiculous without being cheated on—
How can I speak to my betters without stammering?
I, who have been despicable, utterly despicable,
Despicable in the basest and meanest sense of the word . . .

LÀ-BAS, JE NE SAIS OÙ . . .

The day before a journey, rrrrrring . . .
I don't need such a shrill reminder!

I want to enjoy the repose of the station that's my soul
Before I see the iron arrival of the definitive train
Approaching in my direction,
Before I feel the actual departure in the throat of my stomach,
Before I climb aboard, with feet
That have never learned to control their emotion when it's
    time to depart.

Right now, while smoking in the way station of today,
I feel like still relishing a bit of the old life.
A useless life that's best left behind, that's a prison?
What of it? All the universe is a prison, and a prisoner is a
    prisoner whatever size his cell.
My cigarette tastes like impending nausea. The train has
    already left the other station . . .
Goodbye, goodbye everyone who didn't come to see me off,
Goodbye, my abstract and impossible family!
Goodbye to today! Goodbye, way station! Goodbye, life,
    goodbye!

To remain like a labeled package someone forgot,
In a corner of the waiting area on the other side of the tracks.
To be found by an employee once the train has departed—
"And this? Doesn't this belong to a fellow who just left?"

To remain and merely think of departing,
To remain and be right,
To remain and die less . . .

I go to the future as to a difficult exam.
And if the train never comes and God takes pity on me?

I see myself in the station that until now was just a metaphor.
I'm a perfectly presentable person.
You can tell—they say—that I've lived abroad.
I have the manners of an obviously well-bred man.
I grab my suitcase, rejecting the porter like a harmful vice,
And both hand and suitcase tremble.

To depart!
I'll never return.
I'll never return because there is no return.
The place one returns to is always different,
The station one returns to is never the same.
The people are different, the light is different, the philosophy
    is different.

To depart! My God, to depart! I'm afraid of departing! . . .

We crossed paths on a downtown Lisbon street, and he came
    up to me
In his shabby clothes, with Professional Beggar written all
    over his face,
Drawn to me by an affinity that I also feel for him,
And with a broad, effusive gesture I reciprocally gave him all
    I had
(Except, of course, what was in the pocket where I keep more
    money:
I'm no fool, nor a zealous Russian novelist,
Just a Romantic, and that in moderation . . .).

I feel sympathy for people like him,
Especially when they don't deserve sympathy.
Yes, I too am a beggar and a bum,
And likewise through no one's fault but my own.
To be a beggar and a bum doesn't mean you're a beggar and
    a bum:
It means you're not part of the social ladder,
It means you're unadaptable to life's norms,
To life's real or sentimental norms—
It means you're not a High Court judge, a nine to five
    employee, or a prostitute,
Not genuinely poor or an exploited worker,
Not sick with an incurable disease,
Not thirsty for justice, or a cavalry officer,
Not, in short, within any of those social categories depicted
    by novelists

Who pour themselves out on paper because they have good
    reasons for shedding tears
And who rebel against society because their good reasons
    make them think they're rebels.

No: anything but having good reasons!
Anything but caring about humanity!
Anything but giving in to humanitarianism!
What good is a feeling if there's an external reason for it?

Yes, being a beggar and a bum like me
Isn't just being a beggar and a bum, which is commonplace;
It's being a bum by virtue of being isolated in your soul,
It's being a beggar because you have to beg the days to go by
    and leave you alone.

All the rest is stupid, like Dostoyevsky or Gorky.
All the rest is going hungry or having no clothes.
And even if this happens, it happens to so many people
That it's not worth the trouble to trouble over those it
    happens to.
I'm a beggar and a bum in the truest sense, namely the
    figurative sense,
And I'm wallowing in heartfelt compassion for myself.

Poor Álvaro de Campos!
So isolated in life! So depressed!
Poor guy, sunken in the armchair of his melancholy!
Poor guy, who this very day, with (genuine) tears in his
    eyes
And with a broad, liberal, Muscovite gesture,
Gave all he had—from the pocket where he had little—
To that poor man who wasn't poor, who had professionally
    sad eyes.

Poor Álvaro de Campos, whom nobody cares about!
Poor Álvaro, who feels so sorry for himself!

Yes, the poor guy!
Poorer than many who are bums and bum around
Or who are beggars and beg,
Because the human soul is an abyss.

I should know. Poor guy!

How splendid to be able to rebel at rallies in my soul!
But I'm no fool!
And I don't have the excuse of being socially concerned.
I have no excuse at all: I'm lucid.

Don't try to persuade me otherwise: I'm lucid.
It's like I said: I'm lucid.
Don't talk to me about aesthetics with a heart: I'm lucid.
Shit! I'm lucid.

HOLIDAY RETREAT

The stillness of night in this mountain retreat . . .
The stillness that intensifies
The watchdogs' scattered barking in the night . . .
The silence, accentuated
By a slight buzzing or rustling of something in the
    darkness . . .
Ah, how oppressive all this is!
As oppressive as being happy!
What an idyllic life this would be for somebody else,
With this monotonous buzz or rustle of nothing
Beneath the star-studded sky,
With the barking of dogs punctuating the vast stillness!

I came to rest up,
But I forgot to leave myself at home.
I brought along the deep-seated thorn of consciousness,
The vague nausea, the ill-defined affliction of self-awareness.
Always this anxiety chewed bit by bit,
Like dry dark bread that litters the table with its crumbs.
Always this uneasiness swallowed in bitter sips,
Like the wine of a drunkard not even nausea can deter.
Always, always, always
This poor circulation in my soul,
This blacking out of my sensations,
This . . .

Your slender hands, somewhat pale and somewhat mine,
Lay perfectly still in your lap that day,

As the scissors and thimble of another girl might lie.
You sat there lost in thought, looking at me as into space.
(I remember this so as to have something to think about
    without thinking.)
Suddenly, half sighing, you interrupted what you were being.
You consciously looked at me and said:
"It's a pity every day can't be like this."
Like that day that wasn't anything . . .

Ah, you didn't know,
Fortunately you didn't know,
That the pity is that all days are like this, like this . . .
The pity is that, happily or unhappily,
The soul must enjoy or suffer the profound tedium of
    everything,
Consciously or unconsciously,
Thinking or not yet thinking . . .
That is the pity . . .
I photographically remember your listless hands
Lying there, still.
I remember them, in this moment, more than I remember you.
What's become of you?
I know that, in the enormous elsewhere of life,
You married. I presume you're a mother. You're probably
    happy.
Why wouldn't you be?

Only because of some injustice.
Yes, it would be unfair . . .
Unfair?

(It was a sunny day in the fields and I dozed, smiling.)
. . . .
Life . . .
White wine or red, it's all the same: it's to throw up.

No, it's not weariness . . .
It's heaps of disillusion
Contaminating how I think,
It's an upside-down Sunday
Of feeling,
A holiday spent in the abyss . . .

No, it isn't weariness . . .
It's the fact I exist
And the world too,
With everything in it,
With everything in it that keeps unfolding
And that's just various identical copies of the same thing.

No. Why call it weariness?
It's an abstract sensation
Of concrete life—
Sort of like a shout
Not uttered,
Sort of like an anxiety
Not suffered,
Or not suffered completely,
Or not suffered like . . .
Yes, or not suffered like . . .
That's it: like . . .

Like what?
If I knew, I wouldn't have this false weariness.

(Ah, blind people singing in the street . . .
One man playing guitar, another on fiddle, and the woman's
   voice
Add up to quite a barrel organ!)

Because I hear, I see.
Okay, I admit it: it's weariness!

FERNANDO PESSOA–
HIMSELF

What I am essentially—behind the involuntary masks of poet, logical reasoner and so forth—is a dramatist. My spontaneous tendency to depersonalization, which I mentioned in my last letter to explain the existence of my heteronyms, naturally leads to this definition. And so I do not evolve, I simply JOURNEY. (. . .) I continuously change personality, I keep enlarging (and here there is a kind of evolution) my capacity to create new characters, new forms of pretending that I understand the world or, more accurately, that the world can be understood.

(FROM A LETTER OF PESSOA DATED 20 JANUARY 1935)

from

SONGBOOK

O church bell of my village,
Each of your plangent tolls
Filling the calm evening
Rings inside my soul.

And your ringing is so slow,
So as if life made you sad,
That already your first clang
Seems like a repeated sound.

However closely you touch me
When I pass by, always drifting,
You are to me like a dream—
In my soul your ringing is distant.

With every clang you make,
Resounding across the sky,
I feel the past farther away,
I feel nostalgia close by.

8 April 1911

ABDICATION

O night eternal, call me your son
And take me into your arms.
                                        I'm a king
Who relinquished, willingly,
My throne of dreams and tedium.

My sword, which dragged my weak arms down,
I surrendered to strong and steady hands,
And in the anteroom I abandoned
My shattered scepter and crown.

My spurs that jingled to no avail
And my useless coat of mail
I left on the cold stone steps.

I took off royalty, body and soul,
And returned to the night so calm, so old,
Like the landscape when the sun sets.

JANUARY 1913

Swamps of yearnings brushing against my gilded soul . . .
Distant tolling of Other Bells . . . The blond wheat paling
In the ashen sunset . . . My soul is seized by a bodily chill . . .
How forever equal the Hour! . . . The tops of the palms
    swaying! . . .
The leaves staring at the silence inside us . . . Wispy autumn
Of a hazy bird's singing . . . Stagnant, forgotten blue . . .
How quiet the shout of yearning that gives this Hour claws!
How my self-dread longs for something that doesn't weep!
My hands reach out to the beyond, but even as they're
    reaching
I see that what I desire is not what I want . . .
Cymbals of Imperfection . . . O distantly ancient Hour
Banished from its own Time-self! Receding wave that invades
My ceaseless retreating into myself until I faint,
So intent on the present I that I seem to forget myself! . . .
Liquid of halos with no Was behind it, no Self inside it . . .
The Mystery smacks of my being other . . . Bursting in the
    moonlight . . .
The sentry stands very straight, but his lance planted on the
    ground
Is still taller than he . . . What's all this for? . . . The flat
    day . . .
Climbing vines of absurdity tickling Beyonds with this
    Hour . . .
Horizons shutting our eyes to space, where they are false
    links . . .

Opium fanfares of future silences . . . Faraway trains . . .
Gates in the distance . . . seen through the trees . . . so utterly
　　iron!

29 MARCH 1913

from

SLANTING RAIN

I

My dream of an infinite port crosses this landscape
And the flowers' color is transparent to the sails of large ships
Casting off from the wharf, dragging the silhouettes of these
    old
Sunlit trees as their shadows over the waters . . .

The port I dream of is dusky and pallid,
While the landscape is sunny viewed from this side . . .
But in my mind today's sun is a dusky port
And the ships leaving the port are these sunlit trees . . .

Freed into two, I slid straight down the landscape . . .
The substance of the wharf is the clear and calm road
That rises, going up like a wall,
And the ships pass through the trunks of the trees
In a vertically horizontal fashion,
Dropping their moorings through the leaves one by
    one . . .

I don't know who I dream I am . . .
Suddenly all the seawater in the port is transparent
And I see on the bottom, like a huge print unrolled across it,
This entire landscape, a row of trees, a road glowing in that
    port,
And the shadow of a sailing ship older than the port and
    passing

Between my dream of the port and my looking at this
    landscape,
And it approaches me, enters me,
And passes to the other side of my soul . . .

III

The Great Sphinx of Egypt dreams inside this sheet of
    paper . . .
I write—and it appears to me through my transparent hand,
While the pyramids rise up in a corner of the paper . . .

I write—and I'm startled to see that the nib of my pen
Is the profile of King Cheops . . .
I freeze . . .
Everything goes dark . . . I fall into an abyss made of time . . .
I'm buried under the pyramids writing verses by the bright
    light of this lamp
And the whole of Egypt weighs on me through my pen
    strokes . . .
I hear the Sphinx laughing to itself
The sound of my pen running over the paper . . .
An enormous hand, passing through my not being able to
    see it,
Sweeps everything into the corner of the ceiling that's
    behind me,
And on the paper where I write, between it and the pen
    that's writing,
Lies the corpse of King Cheops, looking at me with
    wide-open eyes,
And between our gazing at each other flows the Nile,
And a gaiety of flag-bedecked ships meanders
In a hazy diagonal line
Between me and what I'm thinking . . .

Funeral of King Cheops in old gold and Me! . . .

V

Outside a whirlwind of sun the horses of the merry-go-
    round . . .
Within me a static dance of trees, stones and hills . . .
Absolute night in the brightly lit fair, moonlight on the sunny
    day outside,
And the fair's many lights make noises out of the garden
    walls . . .
Groups of girls with jugs on their heads
Passing by outside and drenched by the sun
Cut across thick crowds of people at the fair,
People mixed up with the lights of the stands, with the night
    and the moonlight,
And the two groups meet and blend
Until they form just one which is both . . .
The fair, the fair lights, the people at the fair
And the night that seizes the fair and lifts it into the air
Can be seen above the tops of the sun-drenched trees,
They're visible beneath the rocks that gleam in the sun,
They loom behind the jugs carried on the girls' heads,
And the whole of this spring landscape is the moon above the
    fair,
And the whole fair, with its sounds and lights, is the ground
    of this sunny day . . .

Suddenly someone shakes this twofold hour as if in a sieve,
And the powder of the two realities, mixed together, falls
On my hands full of drawings of ports
Where huge sailing ships are casting off with no intention of
    returning . . .
Powder of white and black gold on my fingers . . .
My hands are the steps of that girl leaving the fair,
Alone and contented like this day . . .

[1914]

THE REAPER

She sings, poor reaper, believing
She's happy perhaps. She sings,
She reaps, and her voice, full
Of widowed, glad anonymity,

Wavers like the song of a bird
In the air as clean as a threshold,
And the gentle weave of her song
Twists this way and that.

Hearing her cheers and saddens,
The field and its toil are in her voice,
And she sings as if she had
More reasons than life for singing.

Ah, sing, sing for no reason!
In me what feels is always
Thinking. Pour into my heart
Your waving, uncertain voice!

Ah, to be you while being I!
To have your glad unconsciousness
And be conscious of it! O sky!
O field! O song! Knowledge

Is so heavy and life so brief!
Enter inside me! Make

My soul your weightless shadow!
And take me with you, away!

[1914]

SOME RANDOM VERSES

Live with nostalgia for the moment
          Even as you live it . . .
Empty boats, blown ever forward
          Like loose strands of hair
By a long and steady wind, we live
Without knowing what we feel or want . . .

Let's make ourselves aware of this
          As of a still pond
In the midst of a torpid landscape
          Under a desolate sky,
And may our self-awareness
No longer be roused by desire . . .

In this way, equal to the whole hour
          In all its sweetness,
Our life, no longer us, will be
          Our pre-wedding: a color,
A fragrance, a swaying of trees,
And death won't come early or late . . .

What matters is that nothing matter
          Anymore . . . Whether Fate
Hangs over us or quietly and obscurely
          Lurks in the distance
Is all the same . . . Let's be what is:
The moment . . . What good is thinking?

11 OCTOBER 1914

PASSERBY

I hear a piano playing, and laughter
        Behind the music. I pause
In my dreaming to look up: it's from
        The tall building's second floor.

So much joy in those young voices!
        It's false? How do I know?
Their pleasure makes me shiver with envy!
        It's banal? I have no pleasure.

They may be happy on the second floor
        Of that tall building. I
Pass by, dreaming of that home as if
        Dreaming of another country.

24 JUNE 1915

DIARY IN THE SHADE

Do you still remember me?
You knew me a long time ago.
I was that sad child you didn't care for
But then gradually got to be interested in
(In his anguish, his sadness, and something else)
And ended up liking, almost without realizing it.
Remember? The sad Child who played on the beach
By himself, quietly, far away from the others,
And he sometimes glanced at them sadly but without
    regret . . .
I see that you occasionally steal a glance at me.
Do you remember? Do you want to see if you remember?
    I know . . .
Don't you still sense in my sad and calm face
The sad child who always played far away from the others
And sometimes gazed at them with sad eyes but without
    regret?
I know you look at me and don't understand what sadness
    it is
That makes me sad.
It isn't regret or nostalgia, disappointment or resentment.
No . . . It's the sadness
Of one who, in the great prenatal realm,
Must have received from God the Secret—
The secret of the world's illusion,
Of the absolute emptiness of things—
The incurable sadness
Of one who realizes that everything's pointless, worthless,

That effort is an absurd waste,
And that life is a void,
Since disillusion always follows on the heels of illusion
And Death seems to be the meaning of Life . . .
It's this, but not only this, that you see in my face
And that makes you steal an occasional glance at me.
There is, besides this,
That grim astonishment, that black chill,
Which comes from the soul
Having been told a secret of God
In the prenatal realm, when life
Had still shown no sign of dawning
And the whole of the complex, luminous Universe
Was an inevitable destiny yet to be fulfilled.
If this doesn't define me, nothing defines me.
And this doesn't define me—
Because the Secret that God told me wasn't only this.
There was something else, which led to my embracing
The unreal dimension, my delighting in it so much, my knack
For grasping the ungraspable and for feeling what can't be
    felt,
My inward dignity of an emperor, though I have no empire,
My world of dreams fashioned in broad daylight . . .
Yes, that is what gives
My face an oldness even older than my childhood,
And my gaze an anxiety within my happiness.
You occasionally steal a glance at me,
And you don't understand me,
And you steal another glance, and another, and another . . .
Without God there's nothing but life
And you'll never be able to understand . . .

17 SEPTEMBER 1916

A piano on my street . . .
Children playing outside . . .
A Sunday, and the sun
Shining golden with joy . . .

My sorrow that makes me
Love all that's indefinite . . .
Though I had little in life,
It pains me to have lost it.

But my life already
Runs deep in changes:
A piano I miss hearing,
Those children I miss being!

25 FEBRUARY 1917

Where's my life going, and who's taking it there?
Why do I always do what I didn't want to?
What destiny in me marches onward in the darkness?
What part of me that I don't know is my guide?

My destiny has a direction and a method,
My life adheres to a path and a scale,
But my self-awareness is the sketchy outline
Of what I do and am; it's not me.

I don't even know myself in what I knowingly do.
I never reach the end of what I do with an end in mind.
The pleasure or pain I embrace isn't what it really is.
I move on, but there's no I inside me that moves.

Who am I, Lord, in your darkness and your smoke?
What soul besides mine inhabits my soul?
Why did you give me the feeling of a path
If the path I seek I'm not seeking, if in me nothing walks

Except through an effort in my steps that's not mine,
Except by a fate hidden from me in my acts?
Why am I conscious if consciousness is an illusion?
What am I between "what" and the facts?

Close my eyes, obscure my soul's vision!
O illusions! Since I know nothing about life or myself,

May I at least enjoy that nothing, without faith
but calmly,
And at least sleep through life, like a forgotten
beach . . .

5 JUNE 1917

Ah! the anguish, the vile rage, the despair
Of not being able to express
With a shout, an extreme and bitter shout,
The bleeding of my heart!

I speak, and the words I say are mere sound.
I suffer, and it's just me.
Ah! If I could only wrest from music the secret
Timbre of its shout!

What rage that my sorrow can't even shout,
That its shout goes no further
Than the silence, which returns, in the air
Of the night filled with nothing!

15 JANUARY 1920

NON NECESSE EST

It's a stage—a stage in a dream—
With actors but no assigned roles.
There a smiling destiny
Fuses dreaming with being.

Dreamed scenery, deceive him!
Action, don't take place!
Fool the one who made you,
O fictions of the interlude!

And may the soul live in ethereal
Detachment, forgetting about life,
Which is womanish and plebeian,
And death, which isn't anything!

[1921?]

Whoever, horizon, passes beyond you
Passes from view, not from living or being.
Don't call the soul dead when it flies away.
Say: It vanished out there in the sea.

Be for us, sea, the symbol of all life—
Uncertain, unceasing, and more than our seeing!
Once Earth makes its circle and death its journey,
The ship and the soul will reappear.

11 JANUARY 1922

NOTHING

Ah, the soft, soft playing,
Like someone about to cry,
Of a song that's woven
Out of artifice and moonlight . . .
Nothing to make us remember
          Life.

A prelude of courtesies
Or a smile that faded . . .
A cold garden in the distance . . .
And in the soul that finds it,
Just the absurd echo of its empty
          Flight.

8 NOVEMBER 1922

I don't know who I am right now. I dream.
Steeped in feeling myself, I sleep. In this
Calm hour my thought forgets its thinking,
        My soul has no soul.

If I exist, to know it is to err. If I
Wake up, it seems I've strayed. I'm in the dark.
There's nothing I want, have, or remember.
        I have no being or law.

A moment of consciousness between illusions,
I'm bounded all around by phantoms.
Sleep on, oblivious to other people's hearts,
        O heart belonging to no one!

                                6 JANUARY 1923

I hear the wind blowing in the night.
I sense, high up in the air, the whip
Of I don't know whom hitting I don't know what.
Everything's heard; nothing's seen.

Ah, everything is symbol and analogy.
The wind that blows and this cold night
Are something other than night and wind—
They're shadows of Being and of Thought.

Things tell us through stories what they don't say.
I don't know what drama I ruined by thinking—
A drama the night and the wind were telling.
I heard it. Thinking about it, I heard in vain.

Everything softly hums, the same.
The wind stops blowing, the night advances,
Day begins and I exist, anonymous.
But what happened was much more than this.

24 SEPTEMBER 1923

THE SCAFFOLD

The time I've spent dreaming—
Years and years of my life!
Oh, how much of my past
Was only the false life
Of a future I imagined!

Here, alongside the river,
I grow calm for no reason.
Its empty flowing, cold
And anonymous, mirrors
The life I've lived in vain.

How little hope ever attains!
What longing is worth the wait?
Any child's ball
Rises higher than my hope,
Rolls farther than my longing.

Waves of the river, so slight
That you aren't even waves,
The hours, days and years
Pass quickly—mere grass or snow
That die under the same sun.

I spent all I didn't have.
I'm older than I am.
The illusion that kept me going

Was a queen only on stage:
Costume off, her reign ended.

Soft sound of these slow waters
Yearning for shores you've passed,
How drowsy are the memories
Of misty hopes! What dreams
All dreaming and life amount to!

What did I make of my life?
I found myself when already lost.
Impatient, I let myself be,
As one might let a lunatic go on
Believing what's been disproven.

Dead sound of these gentle waters
That flow because they must,
Take not only my memories
But also my dead hopes—
Dead, because they must die.

I'm already my future corpse.
Only a dream links me to myself—
The hazy and belated dream
Of what I should have been—a wall
Around my abandoned garden.

Take me, passing waves,
To the oblivion of the sea!
Bequeath me to what I won't be—
I, who raised a scaffold
Around the house I never built.

29 AUGUST 1924

GLOSSES

1.

Every work is in every way futile.
The futile wind, stirring up futile leaves,
Describes our effort and our general state.
Given or achieved, everything is Fate.

Calmly observe, above your own self,
Lonely and infinite Possibility,
Which uselessly gives rise to what's real.
Hush and, unless it's to think, don't feel.

2.

Neither good nor evil defines the world.
Oblivious to both, the Fate we call God
From the heaven we suppose is "on high"
Rules neither well nor badly earth and sky.

We go through life laughing and crying,
The one state being a contracted face,
And the other some water with a little salt.
Beyond good and evil, Fate decides all.

3.

The sun plies the sky's twelve signs,
Forever rising and forever dying
In the horizons of what we see. Reality,
As we know it, is where we happen to be.

Fictions of our own consciousness,
We've laid instinct and knowledge to rest.
And the sun, unmoving, doesn't even ply
The twelve signs that aren't in the sky.

14 AUGUST 1925

CHESS

Pawns, they go out into the peaceful night,
Tired and full of fictitious feelings.
They're going home, talking about nothing,
Dressed in furs, coats and pelisses.

As pawns, destiny only allows them
One forward square per move, unless
They're given another one diagonally,
On a new path, through someone else's death.

Eternal subjects of the noble pieces,
Like the bishop or rook, that move far and fast,
They're suddenly overtaken by fate
In their lonely march, and breathe their last.

One or another, making it all the way,
Redeems not his own but someone else's life.
And the game goes on, indifferent to each piece,
The relentless hand moving them all alike.

Then, poor creatures dressed in furs or silks,
Checkmate! the game's over and the weary hand
Stows away the contest's meaningless pieces,
Since, just a game, it's nothing in the end.

1 NOVEMBER 1927

How long it's been, ten years perhaps,
        Since I've passed by this street!
And yet I lived here for a time—
        About two years, or three.

The street's the same, with almost nothing new.
        But if it could see me and comment,
It would say, "He's the same, but how I've changed!"
        Thus our souls remember and forget.

We pass by streets and by people,
        We pass our own selves, and we end;
Then, on the blackboard, the Intelligent Hand
        Erases the symbol, and we start again.

12 MARCH 1928

Amidst my anguish over who I am
A thought lifts its brow straight up,
Like a tower. In the vast solitude
Of a soul all alone it's as if
My heart had knowledge and a brain.

I consist of an artificial bitterness,
Faithful to I don't know what idea.
Like a make-believe royal attendant,
I don the fine robes in which I exist
For the artificial presence of the king.

Yes, all I am and want are but dreams.
Everything slipped out of my slack hands.
Arms at my sides, I hopelessly wait—
A beggar who, reduced to despair,
Would ask for charity but doesn't dare.

26 JULY 1930

The harmonium faintly, dyingly whines
         Somewhere in the shapeless dark.
Oh, how these chance strains of music
         Cut to the quick of one's heart!

Waving trees, rising sea, eerie stillness
         Of rushes, a guitar, a voice's moan—
All of this reaches the soul in its depths,
         Where it's completely alone!

When these sounds hurt and there is no love,
         How hazy our essence feels!
Cease, O fluid consciousness!
         Be shadow, O heartfelt grief!

                              4 AUGUST 1930

Whether I'm happy or sad? . . .
Frankly I don't know.
What does it mean to be sad?
What is happiness good for?

I'm neither happy nor sad.
I don't really know what I am.
I'm just one more soul that exists
And feels what God has ordained.

So then, am I happy or sad?
Thinking never ends well . . .
For me sadness means
Hardly knowing myself . . .

But that's what happiness is . . .

20 AUGUST 1930

I want to be free and insincere,
With no creed, duty, or titled post.
I loathe all prisons, love included.
Whoever would love me, please don't!

When I cry about what happened
And sing about what isn't false,
It's because I've forgotten what I feel
And suppose I'm someone else.

A wanderer through my own being,
I pull songs from out of the breeze,
And my errant soul is itself
A song for singing on journeys.

Because a great and calming effect
Of nothing having a reason to be
Falls from the vacant sky like a right
Onto the worthless earth like a duty.

Dead rain from the now clear sky still soaks
The nocturnal ground, and I, just in time,
Beneath my wet clothes, assume the role
Of one or another social type.

26 AUGUST 1930

My wife, whose name is Solitude,
Keeps me from being glum.
Ah, what good it does my heart
To have this nonexistent home!

Returning there, I hear no chatter,
I don't suffer the insult of a hug,
And I talk out loud to no one at all:
My poems take shape as I go.

Lord, if there's some good that Heaven,
Though subject to Fate, can still grant,
Then let me be alone—a fine silk robe—
To talk by myself—a lively fan.

27 AUGUST 1930

Her very being surprises.
A tall, tawny blonde,
It delights me just to think
Of seeing her half-ripe body.

Her tall breasts resemble
(Or would, were she lying down)
Two hills in the early morning,
Even if it isn't dawn.

And the hand of her naked arm
Rests with spread fingers
On the curved, bulging flank
Of her clothed figure.

She entices like a boat,
Or like an orange, so sweet.
When, my God, will I sail?
When, O hunger, will I eat?

10 SEPTEMBER 1930

There's no one who loves me.
Hold on, yes there is;
But it's hard to feel certain
About what you don't believe in.

It's not out of disbelief
That I don't believe, for I know
I'm well liked. It's my nature
Not to believe no matter what.

There's no one who loves me.
For this poem to exist
I have no choice
But to endure this grief.

How sad not to be loved!
My poor, forlorn heart!
Et cetera, and that's the end
Of this poem I thought up.

What I feel is another matter . . .

25 DECEMBER 1930

O cat playing in the street
As if it were a bed,
I envy you your luck,
Because it isn't luck at all.

Servant of the fatal laws
Governing stones and people,
You're ruled by natural instinct
And feel only what you feel.

That's why you're happy.
The nothing that's you is all yours.
I look at myself but I'm missing.
I know myself: it's not me.

JANUARY 1931

I come to the window
To see who's singing.
A blind man and his guitar
Are out there weeping.

Both sound so sad . . .
They form a unity
That roams the world
Making people feel pity.

I'm also a blind man
Who roams and sings.
My road is longer,
And I don't ask for anything.

26 FEBRUARY 1931

AUTOPSYCHOGRAPHY

The poet is a feigner
Who's so good at his act
He even feigns the pain
Of pain he feels in fact.

And those who read his words
Will feel in his writing
Neither of the pains he has
But just the one they're missing.

And so around its track
This thing called the heart winds,
A little clockwork train
To entertain our minds.

1 APRIL 1931

I'm a fugitive.
I was shut up in myself
As soon as I was born,
But I managed to flee.

If people get tired
Of being in the same place,
Why shouldn't they tire
Of having the same self?

My soul seeks me out,
But I keep on the run
And sincerely hope
I'll never be found.

Oneness is a prison.
To be myself is to not be.
I'll live as a fugitive
But live really and truly.

5 April 1931

I'm guided only by reason.
I was given no other guide.
The light it sheds is useless?
I have no other light.

If the world's Creator
Had wanted me to be
Different from how I am,
He'd have made me differently.

He gave me eyes for seeing.
I look, I see, I believe.
How can I dare say:
"Blindness would be a blessing"?

Besides my gaze, God
Gave me reason, for going
Beyond what eyes can see—
The vision we call knowing.

If seeing is being deceived,
And thinking is going astray,
I don't know. God gave them
To me as my truth and way.

2 JANUARY 1932

INITIATION

You aren't asleep under the cypress trees,
For in this world there is no sleep.
. . . .
Your body is the shadow of the clothes
That conceal your deeper self.

When night, which is death, arrives,
The shadow ends without having been.
And you go, unawares, into that night
As the mere outline of yourself.

But at the Inn of Trepidation,
The Angels take away your cape;
You go on with no cape on your shoulders
And little else to cover you.

Then the Highway Archangels
Strip you and leave you naked,
Without any clothes, with nothing:
You have just your body, which is you.

Finally, deep within the cave,
The Gods strip you even more.
Your body, or outer soul, ceases,
But you see that they are your equals.

. . . .

The shadow of your clothes remains
Among us in the realm of Destiny.
You are not dead amid cypress trees.

. . . .

Neophyte, there is no death.

23 MAY 1932

Death is a bend in the road,
To die is to slip out of view.
If I listen, I hear your steps
Existing as I exist.

The earth is made of heaven.
Error has no nest.
No one has ever been lost.
All is truth and way.

23 MAY 1932

Blessed rooster that sings
Of the night that will be day!
It's as if you raised me up
From the self in which I lay.

Your pure and shrill cry
Is the morning before it breaks.
I look forward to the future!
The last star is already faint.

Once more, thank God, I hear
You shout your long, clear sound.
The edge of the sky grows lighter.
Why do I stop and ponder?

19 JUNE 1932

Happy those who don't think, since life
Is their relative and gives them shelter!
Happy those who act like the animals they are!
Better, instead of creeds, to have just faith,
Forgetting who you are or what you want.
Happy those who, unthinking, are true beings,
Since being means to occupy a space
And give consciousness to a place.

29 JUNE 1932

The ancient censer swings,
Its ornate gold full of slits.
Distractedly I concentrate
On the ritual's slow enactment.

But my heart sees and hears
Arms that are invisible,
Songs that aren't being sung,
And censers from other planes.

For when this ritual's performed
With perfect steps and timing,
A ritual from elsewhere awakens,
And the soul's what it is, not seems.

The visible censer swings,
Audible songs fill the air,
But the ritual I'm attending
Is a ritual of what I remember.

In the great prenatal Temple,
Before life, the soul and God . . .
And the chessboard of that ritual floor
Is today the earth and sky . . .

22 SEPTEMBER 1932

What I write's not mine, not mine . . .
Whom do I owe it to?
Whose herald was I born to be?
How was I fooled
Into thinking that what I had was mine?
Who gave it to me?
Whatever the case, if my destiny
Is to be the death
Of another life that lives in me,
Then I, who was
By some illusion this entire
Ostensible life,
Am grateful to the One who lifted me
From the dust I am—
The One for whom I, this upraised dust,
Am just a symbol.

9 NOVEMBER 1932

Everything that exists in the world
Has a history
Except the frogs croaking in the depths
Of my memory.

Every place in the world has somewhere
To be
Except the pond from where this croaking
Is coming.

Within me a false moon rises
Over rushes,
And the pond appears, lit more and less
By the moon.

In what life, where and how, was I
What I remember
Thanks to the frogs croaking in the wake
Of what I forget?

Nothing—just silence dozing among rushes.
At the end
Of my huge old soul the frogs croak
Without me.

13 AUGUST 1933

I don't know if that gentle land
Forgotten on a far-flung, south-sea island
Is reality, a dream, or a mixture
Of dream and life. I know
We yearn for that land. There, there,
Life is young and love smiles.

Perhaps nonexistent palm groves
And distant, impossible alamedas
Give peace and shade to those of us
Who believe that land is attainable.
Us happy? Ah, perhaps, perhaps,
In that land, when that time comes.

But when dreamed of, its luster fades;
Thinking of it, we soon tire of thinking.
Under the palms, by the light of the moon,
We feel the coldness of the moon's glowing.
There just like everywhere, everywhere,
Evil doesn't end, and good can't endure.

Not with islands at the world's end
Nor with palm groves, dreamed or real,
Will our soul cure its deep malaise
Or goodness enter into our heart.
Everything's in us. It's there, there,
That life is young and love smiles.

30 AUGUST 1933

Between my sleeping and dreaming,
Between me and the one in me
Who I suppose I am,
A river flows without end.

In its meandering journeys,
Such as all rivers make,
It passed by other, different
Shores in far-off places.

It arrived at where I now live,
At the house I am today.
If I dwell on myself, it passes;
If I wake up, it has already passed.

And the one I feel I am, who dies
In what links me to myself,
Sleeps where the river flows—
That river without end.

11 SEPTEMBER 1933

The master without disciples
Had a flawed machine
Which, despite all its levers,
Never did anything.

It served as a barrel organ
When no one was there to hear it.
When quiet, it looked liked a curious
Object, but no one came near it.

My soul, rather like
That machine, is flawed.
It's complicated and erratic,
And serves no purpose at all.

13 DECEMBER 1933

SENHOR SILVA

The barber's son passed away,
A child of just five years.
I know his father—for a year now
We've talked as he shaves my beard.

When he told me the news, as much
Heart as I have gave a shudder;
All flustered, I hugged him,
And he wept on my shoulder.

In this calm and stupid life,
I never know how I should act.
But, my God, I feel human pain!
Don't ever deny me that!

28 MARCH 1934

I daydream, far from my cozy
Self-awareness as a man.
I don't know who my soul is,
Nor does it know who I am.

Understand it? It would take time.
Explain it? Don't know if I can.

And in this misunderstanding
Between who I am and what is I
There's a whole other meaning
Lying between earth and sky.

In that gap is born the universe
With suns and stars past counting.
It has a profound meaning,
Which I know. It's outside me.

31 MARCH 1934

Yes, at last a certain peace . . .
A certain ancient awareness,
Felt in life's very substance,
Which tells me the soul won't end,
No matter what road it follows . . .

Facile vision?
A belief shared by many? No,
Because what I feel is different.
It's a life, not a belief . . .
It's not the skin but the heart.

Sun setting in the west, I know
I'll see a different sun tomorrow—
Different, yet the same, in the east.
All is illusion, but nothing lies:
The Nothing that's everything is Being.

31 MARCH 1934

In the peace of night, full of so much enduring
And of books I've read,
Reading them while dreaming, feeling and musing,
Scarcely seeing them,

I raise my head that's suddenly dazed
By this useless reading,
And I see there's peace in the night now ending,
But not in my heart.

As a child I was different . . . To become what I am,
I grew up and forgot.
What I have today is a silence, a law.
Have I won or lost?

[APRIL 1934]

All beauty is a dream, even if it exists,
For beauty is always more than it is.
The beauty I see in you
Isn't here, next to me.

What I see in you lives where I dream,
Far away from here. If you exist,
I only know it
Because I just dreamed it.

Beauty is a music which, heard
In dreams, overflowed into life.
But not exactly into life:
Into the life that dreamed.

22 APRIL 1934

Rolling wave that returns,
Smaller, to the sea that brought you,
Scattering as you retreat,
As if the sea were nothing—

Why, on your return journey,
Do you take only your dissolution?
Why not take as well
My heart to that ancient sea?

I've had it for such a long time
That I'm tired of having to feel it.
So take it in that faint murmur
By which I hear you fleeing!

9 MAY 1934

In this world where we forget,
We are shadows of who we are,
And the real actions we perform
In the other world, where we live as souls,
Are here wry grins and appearances.

Night and confusion engulf
Everything we know down here:
Projections and scattered smoke
From that fire whose glow is invisible
To the eyes we're given by life.

But a few rare people, looking
Closely, can see for a moment
In the shadows and their shifting
The purpose in the other world
Of the actions that make them live.

Thus they discover the meaning
Of what down here are just grins,
And their gaze's intuition
Returns to their far-off body,
Imagined and understood.

Homesick shadow of that body,
Though a lie, it feels the thread

Connecting it to the sublime
Truth that avidly casts it
On the ground of space and time.

9 MAY 1934

Seagulls are flying close to the ground.
They say this means it's going to rain.
But it's not raining yet. Right now
There are seagulls close to the ground
Flying—that's all.

Likewise, when there's happiness,
They say sadness is on its way.
Perhaps, but so what? If today
Is full of happiness, where
Does sadness fit in?

It doesn't. It belongs to tomorrow.
When it comes, then I'll be sad.
Today is pure and good. The future
Doesn't exist today. There's a wall
Between us and it.

Enjoy what you have, drunk on being!
Leave the future in its place.
Poems, wine, women, ideals—
Whatever you want, if it's what is,
Is for you to enjoy.

Tomorrow, tomorrow . . . Be, tomorrow,
What tomorrow brings you. For now

Accept, be ignorant, and believe.
Keep close to the ground, but flying,
Like the seagull.

18 MAY 1934

The beautiful, wondrous fable
Which they told me long ago
Still slumbers in my soul
But is a different fable now.

Back then the fable told
Of fairies, gnomes and elves;
Now it tells only about
Our slavishly wavering selves.

But, when properly considered,
Aren't elves, fairies and gnomes
Just the mistaken projections
Of a wavering that's all our own?

We create what we don't have
Because we're sorry it's missing,
And whatever we long to see
Is what we end up seeing.

Later, tired of that vision
Which sees only what's unreal,
We shut up all the windows
And in our souls are sealed.

Although the vision is gone,
The figures that took part

Still dance, and in great number,
But only inside our heart.

9 JUNE 1934

When I die and you, meadow,
Become something strange to me,
There will be better meadows
For the better self I'll be.

And the flowers that are beautiful
In the fields I see down here
Will be stars of many colors
In the vast fields there.

And perhaps my heart, seeing
That other nature, more natural
Than the vision that fooled us
Into thinking it was real,

Will, like a bird at last alighting
On a branch, look back and recall
This flight of existence
As nothing at all.

2 JULY 1934

There were people who loved me,
There were people I loved.
Today I blushed
Because of who I once was.

I felt ashamed
Of being, here and now,
The one who always dreams
And never steps out,

Ashamed of realizing
That I can have no more
Than this dream of what
I could have been—before.

6 AUGUST 1934

ADVICE

Surround who you dream you are with high walls.
In the part of the yard that can be seen
Through the iron bars of the gate,
Plant only the most cheerful flowers,
So that you'll be known as a cheerful sort.
In the part no one sees, don't plant anything.

Lay flower beds, like other people have,
So that passing gazes can look in
At your garden as you're going to show it.
But where you're all your own and no one
Ever sees you, let wildflowers spring up
Spontaneously, and let the grass grow naturally.

Make yourself into a well-guarded
Double self, letting no one who looks in
See more than a garden of who you are—
A showy but private garden, behind which
The native flora brushes against the grass,
So straggly that not even you see it . . .

10 AUGUST 1934

AT THE TOMB OF
CHRISTIAN ROSENKREUTZ

We had still not seen the corpse of our wise and prudent
Father, and so we moved the altar to one side. Then we
could raise a strong plate of yellow metal, and there lay a
beautiful, illustrious body, whole and uncorrupted . . . , and
in his hand he held a small parchment book, written in gold
and entitled T., which, after the Bible, is our greatest trea-
sure, one that should not be lightly submitted to the world's
censure.

FAMA FRATERNITATIS ROSEAE CRUCIS

I

When, awakened from this sleep called life,
We find out who we are and what
This fall into Body was, this descent
Into the Night that obstructs our Soul,

Will we finally know the hidden
Truth about all that exists or flows?
No: not even the freed Soul knows it.
Nor does God, who created us, contain it.

God is the Man of a yet higher God.
A Supreme Adam, He also fell.
Our Creator, He was also created

And was cut off from the Truth. The Abyss,
His Spirit, hides it from Him in the beyond.
In the World, His Body, it doesn't exist.

II

Before all that there was the Word, here lost
When the already extinguished Infinite Light
Was raised from Chaos, the ground of Being,
Into Shadow, and the absent Word was obscured.

But though it feels its form is wrong, the Soul sees
At last in itself—mere Shadow—the glowing
Word of this World, human and anointed,
The Perfect Rose, crucified in God.

Lords, then, on the threshold of the Heavens,
We may search beyond God for the Secret
Of our Master and the higher Good;

Wakened from here and from ourselves, at last
We're freed in the present blood of Christ
From the World's creation dying to God.

III

Ah, but here where we still wander, unreal,
We sleep what we are, and although in dreams
We may indeed see the truth, we see it
(Since our seeing is a dream) distortedly.

Shadows seeking bodies, how will we feel
Their reality if we find them?
What, as Shadows, can our shadowy hands touch?
Our touch is absence and vacancy.

Who will free us from this closed Soul?
We can hear, if not see, beyond the hall
Of being, but how make the door swing open?

. . . .

Lying before us, calm in his false death
And with the shut Book pressed against his chest,
Our Rosy Cross Father knows, and says nothing.

[1934?]

The girls go in groups
Down the road, singing.
They sing old songs,
The kind that make us cry
When they come to mind.

They sing just to sing,
Because other girls have sung . . .
And the song they've remembered,
Singing it without letup,
Is forever old and present.

In the warm, boisterous sound
There's something eternal
—Life, joy, their girlishness—
That brings to the windows
The girls who don't sing,

The girls who, in the shadow
Of promised or hoped-for love,
Hear their own pained voice
Contained in the lyrics
Laughed and shouted outside.

Yes, that song passing by
Inadvertently expresses
The great and human tragedy

Of loving or not loving—
The same endless tragedy . . .

18 AUGUST 1934

Since night was falling and I expected no one,
I bolted my door against the world,
And my peaceful, humble home
Sank with me into a deep silence . . .

Drunk on aloneness, talking to myself,
Strolling about without a care,
I was that good and true friend
I can no longer find in the friends I have.

But someone suddenly knocked at the door,
And an entire poem went up in smoke . . .
It was the neighbor, reminding me
About lunch tomorrow. Yes, I'll be there.

Once more bolting my door and myself,
I tried to resurrect in my heart
The stroll, the enthusiasm and the desire
That had made me drunk on what other people are.

In vain . . . Just the same furniture as always
And the inevitable walls staring at me,
Like a man who stopped looking at a dying fire
And saw no more fire when he looked again.

19 AUGUST 1934

If someday someone knocks at your door,
Saying that he's my emissary,
Don't believe it, even if it's me,
Since my lofty pride won't even consent
To knocking at the unreal door of heaven.

But if, without hearing anyone knock,
You should happen to open the door
And find someone there who seems to be waiting
For the courage to knock, consider. That
Was my emissary, and me, and what
My finally desperate pride will allow.
Open your door to the man who doesn't knock!

5 SEPTEMBER 1934

Everything, except boredom, bores me.
I'd like, without being calm, to calm down,
To take life every day
Like a medicine—
One of those medicines everybody takes.

I aspired to so much, dreamed so much,
That so much so much made me into nothing.
My hands grew cold
From just waiting for the enchantment
Of the love that would warm them up at last.

Cold, empty
Hands.

6 SEPTEMBER 1934

Tell nothing to the one who told all—
The all that is never all told,
Those words made of velvet
Whose color no one knows.

Tell nothing to the one who bared
Their soul . . . The soul can't be bared.
Confession is made for the calm
It gives us to hear ourselves talk.

Everything is useless, and false.
It's a top that a boy in the street
Sets in motion to see how it spins.
It spins. Tell nothing.

11 OCTOBER 1934

FREEDOM

*All manner of orations and histories, on shelves reaching
up to the ceiling, adorn the home of the lazy man.*

SENECA

Ah, what a pleasure
To leave a task undone,
To have a book to read
And not even crack it!
Reading is a bore,
And studying isn't anything.
The sun shines golden
Without any literature.
The river flows, fast or slow,
Without a first edition.
And the breeze, belonging
So naturally to morning,
Takes its time, it's in no hurry.

Books are just paper painted with ink.
And to study is to distinguish, indistinctly,
Between nothing and not a thing.

How much better, when it's foggy,
To wait for King Sebastian,
Whether or not he ever shows!

Poetry, dancing and charity are great things,
But what's best in the world are children, flowers,
Music, moonlight and the sun, which only sins
When it withers instead of making things grow.

Greater than this
Is Jesus Christ,
Who knew nothing of finances
And had no library, as far as we know . . .

16 MARCH 1935

A gray but not cold day . . .
A day with
Seemingly no patience for being day
And which only on an impulse,
Out of an empty sense
Of duty, tempered with irony,
Finally gives light to a day
Just like me
Or else
Like my heart,
A heart that's empty
Not of emotion
But of pursuing a goal—
A gray but not cold heart.

18 MARCH 1935

What matters is love.
Sex is just an accident:
It can be the same
Or different.
Man isn't an animal:
He's an intelligent flesh,
Though subject to sickness.

5 APRIL 1935

It was such a long time ago!
I don't even know if it was in this life . . .
It's painful to remember it . . .
To be unable to remember it is torture . . .

Yes, it was you,
Or someone who today is you.
Your naked foot rested
On the lion crouched in front of you.

This of course could never
Have happened,
But if it could, it would make life
Less tedious.

Ah, your faraway gaze!
Your lips from back then!
I no longer know how to love them,
Because I've never loved them.

And all of this, which promises
Huge gulfs of emotion,
Is the result of me simply looking at a rug
Which, like everything, lies on the floor.

10 AUGUST 1935

UN SOIR À LIMA

The voice on the radio returns,
Announcing in an exaggerated drawl:
"And now
Un Soir à Lima . . ."

I stop smiling . . .
My heart stops beating . . .

And from the unconscious receiver
That sweet and accursed melody
Breaks forth . . .
My soul loses itself
In a sudden and overwhelming memory . . .

The wooded slope shimmered
Under the great African moon.

The living room in our house was large, and
    everything
Between it and the sea was lit up
By the dark brilliance of that gigantic moon . . .
But only I stood by the window.
My mother was at the piano
And played . . .
That very same
Un Soir à Lima.

My God, how distant and irrevocably lost all that is!
What has become of her noble bearing?
Of her dependably soothing voice?
Of her full and affectionate smile?
What there is today
To remind me of all that
Is this melody, exactly the same melody,
Still playing on the radio,
None other than *Un Soir à Lima*.

Her graying hair was so lovely
In the light,
And I never thought she would die
And leave me at the mercy of who I am!
She died, but I'll always be her little boy,
Because no one, for his mother, is ever a man!

◆

And even through tears my memory
Still preserves
The perfect medallion image
Of that yet more perfect profile.
My forever childish heart weeps
When I remember you, mother, so Roman and already
    graying.
I see your fingers at the keyboard, and the moonlight
Outside shines eternally in me.
In my heart you play, without ceasing,
Un Soir à Lima.

◆

"Did the little ones go right to sleep?"
"Yes, right to sleep."
"This girl here is almost asleep."
And, smiling as you spoke, you continued
Playing,
Attentively playing,
Un Soir à Lima.

All I was when I wasn't anyone,
All I loved and only now know
I loved, now that I have no remotely
Real path, now that I have only
Nostalgia for what was—
It all lives in me
Through lights and music
And my heart's undying vision
Of that eternal hour
In which you turned
The unreal page of music
And I heard and saw you
Continue the eternal melody
That lives today
In the eternal depths of my nostalgia
For the time when you, mother, played
Un Soir à Lima.

And the indifferent receiver
Transmits from the unconscious station
Un Soir à Lima.

I didn't know then that I was happy.
I know it now, because I no longer am.

"This girl here is also sleeping . . ."
"No she isn't."
We all smiled,
And I,
Far from the hard and lonely
Moon that shone outside,
Absentmindedly kept listening
To what made me dream without realizing it,
To what nowadays makes me feel sorry for myself,
That gentle song without voice, just the sounds
Of the keys my mother played:
Un Soir à Lima.

◆

If only I could have that entire scene
Right here, complete and distilled,
Tucked away in a drawer,
Tucked in one of my pockets!
If only I could yank
From space, from time, from life,
That living room, that hour,
The whole family and that peace and that music,
Isolating it all
In some part of my soul
Where I could have it
Forever
Alive, warm,
As real as it is back there
Even now,
When, mother, dear mother, you played
Un Soir à Lima.

Mother, mother, I was your boy
Whom you taught to be
So well-behaved,
And today I'm a rag
Rolled into a ball by Destiny and tossed
Into a corner.

There I pathetically lie,
But the memory of what I heard and what I knew
Of affection, of home and of family
Rises to my heart in a swirl,
And remembering it I heard, today, my God,
   all alone,
Un Soir à Lima.

Where is that hour, that home, that love
When, mother, dear mother, you played
Un Soir à Lima?

And my sister,
Tiny and snuggled up in a stuffed chair,
Didn't know
If she was sleeping or not . . .

◆

I've been so many vile things!
I've been so unfaithful to who I am!
How often my parched,
Subtle reasoner's spirit
Has abundantly erred!
How often even my emotion
Has unfeelingly deceived me!

Since I have no home,
May I at least dwell
In this vision
Of the home I had then.
May I at least listen, listen, listen,
There by the window
Of never again ceasing to feel,
In that living room, our warm
    living room
In capacious Africa where the moon
Outside shines vast and indifferent,
Neither good nor bad,
And where, mother,
In my heart, mother,
You visibly play,
You eternally play
Un Soir à Lima.

◆

My stepfather
(What a man! what heart and soul!)
Reclined his calm and robust
Athlete's body

In the largest chair
And listened, smoking and musing,
His blue eyes without any color.
And my sister, then a child,
Curled up in her chair,
Heard while sleeping
And smiling
That someone was playing
Perhaps a dance . . .

And I, standing before the window,
Saw all the moonlight of all Africa flooding
The landscape and my dream.

Where did all of that go?
Un Soir à Lima . . .
Shatter, heart!

◆

But I'm dizzy.
I don't know if I'm seeing or if I'm sleeping,
If I am who I was,
If I'm remembering or if I'm forgetting.
Something hazily flows
Between who I am and what I was,
And it's like a river, or a breeze,
    or a dream,
Something unexpected
That suddenly stops,
And from the depths where it seemed
    it would end
There emerges, more and more clearly,
In a nimbus of softness and nostalgia
Where my heart still lingers,
A piano, a woman's figure, a longing . . .
I sleep in the lap of that melody,
Listening to my mother play,

Listening, now with the salt of tears on my tongue,
  to *Un Soir à Lima.*

The veil of tears does not blind me.
Crying, I see
What that music gives me—
The mother I had, that home from long ago,
The child I was,
The horror of time because it flows,
The horror of life because it only kills.
I see, and fall asleep,
And in my torpor, forgetting myself,
I see my mother playing the piano.
And those small white hands,
Whose caresses will never again comfort me,
Play carefully and calmly
Un Soir à Lima.

Ah, I see everything clearly!
I'm back there once more.
I turn away my eyes that had been gazing
At the extraordinary moon outside.

But wait, I'm rambling, and the music has ended . . .
I ramble as I've always rambled,
With no inner certainty about who I am,
Nor any real faith or firm rule.
I ramble, I create my own eternities
With the opium of memory and abandon.
I enthrone fantastical queens
Yet have no throne for them to sit on.

I dream because I wallow
In the unreal river of that recollected music.
My soul is a ragged child
Sleeping in a dusky corner.

All I have of my own
In true, waking reality
Are the tatters of my abandoned soul
And my head that's dreaming next to the wall.

Oh isn't there, mother, dear mother,
Some God to save all this from futility,
Some other world in which this lives on?
I continue to ramble: everything is illusion.
Un Soir à Lima . . .

Shatter, heart . . .

17 SEPTEMBER 1935

PEDROUÇOS*

When I was little I didn't know
I'd grow up.
Or I knew but didn't feel it.

Time at that age doesn't exist.
Each day it's the same kitchen table
With the same backyard outside,
And sadness, when felt,
Is sadness, but you aren't sad.

That's how I was,
And all the children in the world
Were that way before me.

A wooden latticework fence,
Tall and fragile,
Divided the huge backyard
Into a vegetable garden and a lawn.

My heart has grown forgetful
But not my eyes. Don't steal from them, Time,

---

*Pedrouços is a neighborhood on the western edge of Lisbon where Pessoa
spent much of his early childhood, at the house of his great-aunt Maria and
great-uncle Cunha. The couple, who had no children, doted on their nephew.

That picture in which the happy boy I was
Gives me a happiness that's still mine!

Your cold flowing means nothing
To a man who cuddles up in memories.

22 OCTOBER 1935

There are sicknesses worse than any sickness;
There are pains that don't ache, not even in the soul,
And yet they're more painful than those that do.
There are anxieties from dreams that are more real
Than the ones life brings; there are sensations
Felt only by imagining them
That are more ours than our very own life.
There are countless things that exist
Without existing, that lastingly exist
And lastingly are ours, they're us . . .
Over the muddy green of the wide river
The white circumflexes of the seagulls . . .
Over my soul the useless flutter
Of what never was nor could be, and it's everything.

Give me more wine, because life is nothing.

19 NOVEMBER 1935

from
MESSAGE

COAT OF ARMS:
THE CASTLES

Europe, stretched out from East to West
And propped on her elbows, stares
From beneath her romantic hair
With Greek eyes, remembering.

Her left elbow is pulled back;
Her right forms an angle.
The first, lying flat, says Italy;
The second says England and extends
The hand that holds up her face.

She stares with a fatal, sphinxian gaze
At the West, the future of the past.

The staring face is Portugal.

8 DECEMBER 1928

COAT OF ARMS: THE SHIELDS

What the Gods give they sell.
The price of glory is adversity.
Pity the happy, for they are only
What is passing!

Let those for whom enough is enough
Have just enough to feel they have enough!
Life is brief, the soul is vast:
Having is procrastinating.

God, by defining Christ
With adversity and disgrace,
Opposed him to Nature
And anointed him Son.

8 DECEMBER 1928

ULYSSES

Myth is the nothing that's everything.
The very sun that breaks through the skies
Is a bright and wordless myth—
God's dead body,
Naked and alive.

This hero who cast anchor here,
Because he never was, slowly came to exist.
Without ever being, he sufficed us.
Having never come here,
He came to be our founder.

Thus the legend, little by little,
Seeps into reality,
Spreading and enriching it.
Life down below, half
Of nothing, perishes.

VIRIATHUS

If souls that feel and act have knowledge
Only by recalling what they'd forgotten,
Our race lives because in us
The memory of your instinct survived.

A nation thanks to your reincarnation,
A people because you resurrected
(You or what you represented)—
That's how Portugal took shape.

Your being is like the cold
Light that precedes daybreak
And is already the stirrings of day
In the dark chaos on the brink of dawn.

22 JANUARY 1934

COUNT HENRY

Every beginning is involuntary.
God is the prime mover.
The hero is his own spectator,
Uncertain and unaware.

You gaze at the sword you found
In your hands.
"What shall I do with this sword?"

You raised it, and it did the doing.

SEBASTIAN, KING OF PORTUGAL

A madman, yes, because I wanted glory
Such as Fortune never grants.
My certainty couldn't fit in me,
And so what I left on those foreign sands
Is the me that I was, not am.

Let others take up my madness
And all that went with it.
Without madness what is man
But a healthy beast,
A postponed corpse that breeds?

20 FEBRUARY 1933

FROM PART TWO / PORTUGUESE SEA

HORIZON

O sea more ancient than us, your terrors
Hid coral, beaches, and forests.
Tearing the veil from night and fog,
From storms withstood and from the unknown,
The ships of initiation saw the Distance
Burst into flower and the South sky shimmer.

As the ship approaches the stark line
Of the coast that, seen from afar, was barren,
A slope with trees emerges. Nearer,
The land breaks into sounds and colors;
And, once ashore, there are birds and flowers
Where just an abstract line had run.

To dream is to see invisible forms
In the hazy distance, and then,
With intuitive thrusts of hope and will,
To seek in that cold horizon trees,
Beaches, flowers, birds, and fountains—
Kisses Truth gives the deserving.

THE COLUMBUSES

Others are bound to have
What we are bound to lose.
Others are apt to find
What in our discoveries
Was found, or not found,
In accord with Destiny.

But what they cannot have
Is the Magic of the Faraway
Which makes it history.
For this reason their glory
Is a tempered brilliance, given
By a borrowed light.

2 APRIL 1934

THE WEST

With two hands—Doing and Destiny—
We unveiled it. While one hand raises
Skyward the flickering, divine torch,
The other pulls the veil away.

Whether the fateful or fortuitous hour
Was the hand that tore the veil from the West,
Science was the soul and Daring the body
Of that unveiling hand.

Whether Chance or Will or Storm
Was the hand that raised the glowing torch,
God was the soul and Portugal the body
Of that torch-bearing hand.

FROM PART THREE / THE HIDDEN ONE

THE FIFTH EMPIRE

Sad the man who lives at home,
Content with his hearth,
Without a dream whose fluttering wing
Makes the embers glow redder
In the warm fire to be abandoned!

Sad the man who is happy!
He lives because life endures.
Nothing in his soul tells him
More than a root can teach:
To have burial for one's life.

Let era after era follow
In the time measured by eras.
To be a man is to be discontent.
Let the vision of his soul
Subdue blind forces!

And when the four great ages
Of the one who dreamed are over,
The earth will be the stage
For the bright day that began
In the gloom of desolate night.

Greece, Rome, Christendom,
Europe—the four ages will go
To where all ages go. Who

Will come to live the truth
That King Sebastian died?

21 FEBRUARY 1933

FOG

No king or law, nor war or peace,
Defines with clarity and substance
The tarnished splendor of the land
That is Portugal wrapped in grief—
Brilliance without light or warmth,
Like the glow of the will-o'-the-wisp.

No one knows what they want.
No one knows their own soul.
No one knows what's good or bad.
(What distant yearning weeps close by?)
All is uncertain and dying.
All is scattered, nothing is whole.
O Portugal, today you are fog . . .

Now is the Hour!

10 DECEMBER 1928

RUBA'IYAT

Dusk shrouds the long and useless day.
Even the hope it denied us crumbles
To nothing . . . Life is a drunken beggar
Holding out his hand to his own shadow.

———

We sleep the universe away. The boundless
Mass of disparate things weaves dreams
In us, and the drunken human confluence
Hollowly echoes from people to people.

———

Pain follows pleasure, which follows pain.
Today we drink wine in celebration,
Tomorrow we'll drink it because we grieve.
But nothing from either wine will remain.

———

Each day gives me cause to hope
For what no day can ever give me.
Each day makes me weary from hoping . . .
But to live is to hope and to grow weary.

Races the color of gold or of copper,
Warmed by the same sun on the same earth,
And no trace of either color will remain
Or be remembered, above or below . . .

———

Already almost forty times
My sun has brought me to the same place
And aged me with the aging felt by all things
Done by Fate, since it also undoes them.

———

Thousands like you are doing their best
To deny their desire for what exists.
Thousands like you, like a person waking up,
Are once more slaves of the endless, vain present.

———

Wise are those who let Destiny mold them.
If I must have glory or misfortune,
It will come without my wanting or doing.
What's to be will be and, having been, passes.

Drink up! Life isn't good or bad.
It gives us what we've given it.
Everything is restored to what wasn't.
And no one knows what it is or will be.

———

Effort lasts as long as faith lasts.
But what lasts, and how long, for one who isn't?
Ah, drink, drink, drink till you forget
How and why, where from and where to!

———

I'm weary of hearing "I'll do this."
Of doing or not doing, who is king?
An animal on whom the soul was foisted,
Man sleeps fitfully. That's all I know.

———

Don't say that the soul lives eternally
Or that the body, once buried, feels nothing.
What can you know about what you don't know?
Drink! You know only the nothing of today.

Leave in a complex state of slumber
Your consciousness of science. Look
At your white face in the wine's red mirror;
Then drink the mirror . . . and your consciousness.

———————

How many kabbalahs I've contemplated!
I can't find them or myself in the end.
Leave the occult in its well and enjoy,
While they last, the sun and your house and garden.

———————

Without hope or desire, love or faith,
Spend your life refusing life, until
It's time to put away your toys and go
To bed. Everything is what it isn't.

———————

However you choose to shape your life,
It was already shaped before you lived it.
Why do you wish to trace on the ground
The fleeing shadow of the passing cloud?

You've died, I weep, and I weep still more,
Because I know why I weep and will weep:
Not from regret that you no longer are
But from regret for when I'll cease to be.

———

All is useless, knowing this included.
Day leads to night, which recreates day.
On the august eve of renunciation,
Renounce renunciation itself.

———

Wise the man who locks up what he's missing,
So that no one will know the nothing he is.
Every mask conceals a skull.
Every soul is the mask of nobody.

———

Don't fret over science or how to use it.
What good, in this dusky room called life,
Will it do you to measure chairs and tables?
Use them, don't measure; you'll soon leave the room.

Let's quietly enjoy the sun while it shines.
After it leaves the sky, let's rest.
When it returns, perhaps it won't find us.
But it could be that we'll also return.

————

Science is heavy, consciousness disquiets,
Art is lame, faith blind and remote.
Life must be lived, and it is useless.
Drink, for the caravan never arrives.

————

Drink! If you listen, you'll hear just the sounds
Of grass or leaves, brought to your ears
By the wind, which is nothing. That's the world:
A regular movement of oblivion.

————

You pick roses? Aren't you just picking
Colorful motifs of death? But pick roses!
Why not pick them, since it pleases you
And everything is its own dissolution?

Twelve times the good-natured sun changes sign
And helps us without any outside help.
We go on living and are who we are
Until death comes to assist who we aren't.

———

The whole of the universe is something else,
And toil, like dead seaweed or fallen leaves,
Floats on the surface of nothing. A slight wind
Stirs the waters a little, and this is life.

———

Exchange for wine the love you won't have.
What you wait for, you'll always wait for.
What you drink, you drink. Look at the roses.
Once you're dead, what roses will you smell?

———

If you, like all visible things, must die,
To live thirty years or a hundred
Is the same. Drink and forget. Spit hope,
Vomit charity, and urinate faith.

Like dust raised up from the road for a moment
By the wind that comes and goes,
The hollow breath of life lifts us up
From nothing, ceases, and returns us to nothing.

———

Waiting is tiresome. Thinking no less so.
Dully and serenely our worthless days
Pass us by without thinking or waiting,
Ever more fatal, and smaller.

———

Life is earth, and living it is mud.
Style, difference, and manner are everything.
In all that you do be only you.
In all that you do be the whole of you.

———

Those who rule rule because they rule,
Whether their rule is good or bad.
Everyone is great when their hour arrives.
Everyone, at heart, is the same nobody.

from
FAUST

The only mystery in the universe
Is that there's a mystery of the universe.
Yes, this sun that unknowingly gives light,
The earth, the trees and all the seasons,
The stones I walk over, the white houses,
People, human fellowship, history,
All that passes—tradition or speech—
Between one soul and another, voices, cities—
None of this has an explanation for why
It exists, much less a mouth for speaking.

Why doesn't the sun come up announcing
What it is? What secret reason explains
The existence of the stones under my feet,
Of the air I breathe, and of my need to breathe?
It's all an absurd and monstrous machine.
We're ignorant with the whole of our body
And our seeing, which is the soul's body.

Why is there anything? Why is there a universe?
Why is this universe the one that exists?
Why is the universe made the way it's made?

Why is there anything? Why is there what is?
Why is there a world, and why is it the world it is?
Why is there "here," "two," consciousness and difference?

————

Monologue in the night

. . .

O lying system of the universe,
Vacuous stars, unreal suns,
The whole of my exiled being hates you
With a physical and vertiginous hatred!
I'm hell in person. I'm the black Christ
Nailed to the fiery cross of myself.
I'm the knowledge that doesn't know,
The insomnia of suffering and thinking
Hunched over the book of the world's horror.

. . .

———

Life's brief and fleeting nature proves
It must be a dream. For me, as the dreamer
Who vaguely feels the regret of knowing
I'll have to wake up, death frightens
Less as death than as the horror
Of it taking away my dream and giving me
Reality.

. . .

———

. . .
Ah, the metaphysical horror of Action!
My gestures break away from me,
And I see them in the air like the vanes
Of a windmill, utterly not mine, and I feel
My life circulating inside them!
I'm always the same, always, always!
Always the one who sees and feels everything
In all its mystery and enormity,
Mystery being the blood of my veins . . .
Always . . . Nothing cures or extinguishes me!
                    If only something
Would abolish my being but not me! . . .

———

The metaphysical dread of Someone Else!
The horror of another consciousness,
Like a god spying on me!
                              How I wish
I were the only consciousness in the universe,
So that no one else's gaze would observe me!

The living mystery of seeing stares at me
From everyone's eyes, and the horror of them
Seeing me is overwhelming.

I can't conceive myself as anyone else,
Nor imagine this consciousness—my twin—
Having any other form, or a differently
Different content. All I see are
People, animals, wild beasts and birds
Horribly alive and staring at me.
I'm like a supreme God who one day
Realized that he's not the only one
And whose infinite gaze now confronts
The horror of other infinite gazes.

Ah, if at least I reflect the transcendent
Glow from beyond God!

———

Today if someone I cherish dies (assuming
Some part of me can still be engrossed
By what's outside me)—if someone I love
(Let's admit the possibility) should die,
I no longer weep or feel grief: I'm chilled,
That's all, by the speechless presence of death,
Which triples my feeling of mystery.

———

Sometimes a song of love rises
To my lips, and I instinctively pine
For a dead beloved—yes,
For the forever dead fiancée of an I
Who couldn't love.
                    Oh, how happy
I'd be if I could annihilate
Thought and emotion (what I most hate
And most cherish) and devote myself
To an empty and toilsome life,
Full of loves and affection! I'd drink water
From the brook of existing without asking
Where it sprang from or where it ends. Joy!
Joy was made for those who can't feel it.
Sheer and palpable horror of the Mystery
Now returns to haunt my thoughts!

When two youthful
Beings fall naturally in love,
Harmonies seem to pour like perfumes
Across the flowering earth,
But the idea of me being in love
Sets off a horrid burst of laughter
Deep down, since I look so ridiculous,
Since I'm so unused to something so natural.
Never, as when I think about love,
Do I feel so foreign and out of place,
So full of hatred for my destiny,
So enraged against life's very essence.
And these sentiments stir up in me
A black cloud of disgust and loathing
That makes the greatest and vilest crimes
Inadequate to convey the humble
And common sordidness of what I feel.

Dialogue in the night

. . .

What metaphysical horror you arouse in me,
Not mentally but viscerally!
O vile metaphysics of the horror of flesh,
The fear of love . . .

Between your body and my desire for it
Stretches the chasm of you being conscious.
If only I could love and possess you
Without you existing or being there!

Ah, my solitary habit of thinking
So exiles the animal in me
That I dare not dare what the vilest creature
Of this vile world does automatically!

I've so concealed my instinctive nature
From human seeing that I don't know
How to reveal, in gestures and manners,
A single instinct to observing eyes,
How to make my body and behavior
Bear witness to who I am! If only
You were blind, O eyes and hands of others!
I don't even know how, in soul or body,
To be naked to others! Eternal solitude . . .

. . .

———

The secret of Seeking is that nothing's found.
Eternal worlds endlessly and unceasingly
Keep spinning in vain, one inside another.
There's us, and the Gods, and the Gods of Gods,
And we're so interspersed and lost in them
That we can't even find ourselves in infinity.
Nothing's ever the same, and the uncertain

Light of supreme truth is always ahead
Of where men and gods go.

————

Ah, everything is symbol and analogy!
The wind that blows and the night that chills
Are something other than night and wind—
Shadows of life and of thought.

Everything we see is something else.
The sweeping tide, the raging tide,
Is the echo of another tide that flows
Where the world is really real.

All we have is forgetfulness.
The cold night and the wind's blowing
Are shadows of the hands whose motions
Are the mother illusion of this illusion.

————

Endlessly condemned to eternal error—
Might not this be our reality? Might not
The abstract and infinitely veiled world
Be an eternal delusion, destined
To remain forever veiled and abstract,
Its very unity an inexactness,
An indefinite whole, and more than a whole,
Where the fixed points of truth and error
Are but a greater error?

————

Everything transcends everything.
Inwardly and infinitely
Far from itself, the universe,
By existing, deceives itself.

————

The supreme mystery of the Universe,
The only mystery at all, and in all,
Is the existence of a mystery of the universe,
It's the existence of the universe, of anything,
It's the existence of existence. O hazy, abstract form
Which existence so often assumes in me,
The mere thought of this is a chill wind in my body
Blowing from beyond the earth and grave
And going from my soul to God.

———

In me

I step up to the brink of myself and look down . . .
An abyss . . . In that abyss the Universe
With its Time and Space is a star, and there are
Other universes in the abyss, other
Forms of Being with other Times and Spaces,
And other lives different from this life . . .
The spirit is also a star . . . The God we ponder
Is a sun . . . And there are more Gods, more spirits
Belonging to other kinds of Reality . . .
I hurl myself into the abyss and remain
In myself . . . And never descend . . . I shut my eyes
And dream, thus returning to Myself and to Life . . .

———

Oh, to drink life in one gulp, a gulp
Containing all of life's sensations
In all their forms, good and bad,
Travails, pleasures and occupations,
All places, journeys, explorations,
All crimes, lusts, and forms of decadence!

In the past I wanted
To revel in trees and flowers,
To dream of cliffs, seas and solitude,
But today I shun that crazy idea:

Anything that brings me close to the Mystery
Racks me with horror. Today I want only
Sensations, lots and lots of sensations,
Of everything and everyone in the world—
Not the sensations of pantheist deliriums
But perpetual shocks of human pleasure,
With my personality always changing
To synthesize them in one stream of feeling.
I want to drown in turmoil, light and voices
—In tumultuously commonplace things—
This feeling of desolation that fills
And overwhelms me.
                    How I would rejoice
To experience in one day, one hour, one gulp
The sum total of all vices, even if
It meant I'd be eternally condemned
—Oh, what madness!—to hell itself!

ENGLISH POEMS

*These poems contain, here and there, certain eccentricities
and peculiarities of expression; do not attribute these to the
circumstance of my being a foreigner, nor indeed consider
me a foreigner in your judgement of these poems. I practice
the same thing, to a far higher degree, in Portuguese. (. . .)*

*The fact is that these are forms of expression necessarily
created by an extreme pantheistic attitude, which, as it
breaks the limits of definite thought, so must violate the
rules of logical meaning.*

(FROM A COVER LETTER SENT BY PESSOA WITH SIXTEEN POEMS
TO AN ENGLISH PUBLISHER ON 23 OCTOBER 1915)

POEMS OF
ALEXANDER SEARCH

EPIGRAM

"I love my dreams," I said, a winter morn,
To the practical man, and he, in scorn,
Replied: "I am no slave of the Ideal,
But, as all men of sense, I love the Real."
Poor fool, mistaking all that is and seems!
I love the Real when I love my dreams.

[1906]

GOD'S WORK

"God's work—how great his power!" said he
As we gazed out upon the sea
Beating the beach tumultuously
    Round the land-head.

The vessel then strikes with a crash,
Over her deck the waters rash
Make horror deep in rent and gash.
    "God's work," I said.

JULY 1906

THE CIRCLE

I traced a circle on the ground,
It was a mystic figure strange
Wherein I thought there would abound
Mute symbols adequate of change,
And complex formulas of Law,
Which is the jaws of Change's maw.

My simpler thoughts in vain had stemmed
The current of this madness free,
But that my thinking is condemnèd
To symbol and analogy:
I deemed a circle might condense
With calm all mystery's violence.

And so in cabalistic mood
A circle traced I curious there;
Imperfect the made circle stood
Though formèd with minutest care.
From Magic's failure deeply I
A lesson took to make me sigh.

30 JULY 1907

A TEMPLE

I have built my temple—wall and face—
Outside the idea of space,
Complex-built as a full-rigged ship;
I made its walls of my fears,
Its turrets many of weird thoughts and tears—
And that strange temple, thus unfurled
Like a death's-head flag, that like a whip
Stinging around my soul is curled,
Is far more real than the world.

AUGUST 1907

from
35 SONNETS

I

Whether we write or speak or are but seen
We are ever unapparent. What we are
Cannot be transfused into word or mien.
Our soul from us is infinitely far.
However much we give our thoughts the will
To make our soul with arts of self-show stored,
Our hearts are incommunicable still.
In what we show ourselves we are ignored.
The abyss from soul to soul cannot be bridged
By any skill or thought or trick for seeing.
Unto our very selves we are abridged
When we would utter to our thought our being.
    We are our dreams of ourselves, souls by gleams,
    And each to each other dreams of others' dreams.

[AUGUST 1910]

VIII

How many masks wear we, and undermasks,
Upon our countenance of soul, and when,
If for self-sport the soul itself unmasks,
Knows it the last mask off and the face plain?
The true mask feels no inside to the mask
But looks out of the mask by co-masked eyes.
Whatever consciousness begins the task
The task's accepted use to sleepness ties.
Like a child frighted by its mirrored faces,
Our souls, that children are, being thought-losing,
Foist otherness upon their seen grimaces
And get a whole world on their forgot causing;
    And, when a thought would unmask our soul's masking,
    Itself goes not unmasked to the unmasking.

[MAY 1912]

XVII

My love, and not I, is the egoist.
My love for thee loves itself more than thee;
Ay, more than me, in whom it doth exist,
And makes me live that it may feed on me.
In the country of bridges the bridge is
More real than the shores it doth unsever;
So in our world, all of Relation, this
Is true—that truer is Love than either lover.
This thought therefore comes lightly to Doubt's door—
If we, seeing substance of this world, are not
Mere Intervals, God's Absence and no more,
Hollows in real Consciousness and Thought.
    And if 'tis possible to Thought to bear this fruit,
    Why should it not be possible to Truth?

9 JULY 1912

XXXI

I am older than Nature and her Time
By all the timeless age of Consciousness,
And my adult oblivion of the clime
Where I was born makes me not countryless.
An exile's yearnings through my thoughts escape
For daylight of that land where once I dreamed,
Which I cannot recall in colour or shape
But haunts my hours like something that hath gleamed
And yet is not as light rememberèd,
Nor to the left or to the right conceived;
And all round me tastes as if life were dead
And the world made but to be disbelieved.
    Thus I my hope on unknown truth lay; yet
    How but by hope do I the unknown truth get?

24 DECEMBER 1912

from

THE MAD FIDDLER

THE LOST KEY

Set out from sight of shore!
　　Grow tired of every sea!
All things are ever more
　　Than most they seem to be.
What steps are those that pass outside my door?

Fail out from shape and thought!
　　Let sense and feeling fade!
O sadness overwrought
　　With joy till bliss is strayed!
What birds are those that my swift window shade?

But be those steps no steps,
　　And be those birds dreamed wings,
Still one ache oversteps
　　The life to which it clings,
Though to know what ache no step in me helps
　　And what this pang is no bird in me sings.

8 FEBRUARY 1913

THE KING OF GAPS

There lived, I know not when, never perhaps—
   But the fact is he lived—an unknown king
Whose kingdom was the strange Kingdom of Gaps.
   He was lord of what is twixt thing and thing,
Of interbeings, of that part of us
     That lies between our waking and our sleep,
      Between our silence and our speech, between
Us and the consciousness of us; and thus
     A strange mute kingdom did that weird king keep
      Sequestered from our thought of time and scene.

Those supreme purposes that never reach
   The deed—between them and the deed undone
He rules, uncrowned. He is the mystery which
   Is between eyes and sight, nor blind nor seeing.
   Himself is never ended nor begun,
Above his own void presence empty shelf.
   All He is but a chasm in his own being,
The lidless box holding not-being's no-pelf.

All think that he is God, except himself.

17 FEBRUARY 1913

NOTES

INTRODUCTION

All the translations are my own. The literary excerpts are taken from the volume in hand, from *Fernando Pessoa & Co.—Selected Poems* (New York: Grove Press, rev. 2022), and from *The Book of Disquiet* (New York and London: Penguin, rev. 2015). Most of the quotations from Pessoa's letters and other writings can be found in *The Selected Prose of Fernando Pessoa* (Grove Press, rev. 2022).

ALBERTO CAEIRO

The Keeper of Sheep. When the editors of the Coimbra-based magazine *Presença*, in which Pessoa published some of his most memorable poems and prose pieces, told him they wanted to publish a volume of his poetry, this was the work he promised to send them. In a letter to one of the editors dated 25 February 1933, he called *The Keeper of Sheep* "the best thing I've done—a work which . . . I could never match, even if I were to write another *Iliad*, for it springs from a type and degree of inspiration (here the word may be used, for it's perfectly accurate) that surpasses what in myself I could rationally generate, which would never be true of any *Iliad*." He expected to deliver the manuscript forthwith, as it needed only some minor revisions. But despite the insistence of the editors, he never got the book into final shape. He published half of its forty-nine poems in magazines, but the other half continued to hesitate, as it were, in a notebook where he kept tinkering, jotting down variant phrasings, adding or subtracting lines, and calling into question certain passages and even entire poems.

The following poems were published in the magazine *Athena* 4, in 1925: IX, XIII, XXVI, XXVIII, XXX, XXXV, XLIII, XLV, XLVI, XLVIII, XLIX. Pessoa, never satisfied, scribbled in pencil some possible revisions to these poems in a copy of *Athena* 4. Since these were clearly changes he was only considering, I have translated the poems as he published them.

II Variants of "My gaze is" in l. 1: "In my gaze everything is"; "Everything I see is." Variants of "completely" in l. 12: "endlessly"; "suddenly." Variant of "supreme" in the penultimate line: "eternal." Variant of "sum of" in the last line: "only."

IV St. Barbara is invoked for protection against storms. Variant of ll. 21–24: "Peacefully listening to the kettle, / With older female relatives for company, / And naturally being this way, like a flower." Variant of "Is a sudden noise / That begins with light . . ." in the penultimate stanza: "Is a bunch of angry / People above us. . . ."

VII Variant of "on top of" in l. 6: "halfway up."

VIII Published in *Presença* 30, in 1931.

XIV Variant of "rarely" in l. 2: "never." Variant of "divine" in l. 5: "natural."

XVI This and the following poem are the only Caeiro poems that rhyme (in the original).

XXI Between the second and third lines, the manuscript contains the following, subsequently added, line, "And if the earth were something to munch on," marked for possible inclusion. Variant of the last line: "That's how it is and how I want it to be. . . ."

XXVII Variant of the last line: "I enjoy it all like someone in the sunlight."

XXXIII Variant of "true" in l. 3: "good." Variant of "coloring" in l. 4: "smile." Variants of the last line: "To see if they talked"; "To see if they moved"; "To see what they would do"; "To see whom they belonged to."

XXXIV Variant of ll. 13–15: "If it is, then well and good . . . / What does it matter to me?"

XXXVI Variant of "true" in l. 7: "artistic."

XLI Variant of l. 5: "In all the leaves of their leaves." Variant of "original" in l. 15: "different." Variant of "bigger" in l. 16: "interesting."

The Shepherd in Love. The Portuguese title for this group of eight poems, *O Pastor Amoroso*, was translated by Pessoa—or, if we like, by an English-language heteronym called Thomas Crosse—as *The*

Lovesick Shepherd. In an unfinished preface to Caeiro's work, Pessoa-qua-Crosse explained: "In the later poems, his lucid inspiration becomes slightly blurred, a little less lucid. The transformation dates from *The Lovesick Shepherd.* Love brought a touch of sentiment into this strangely unsentimental poetry. When that love brought disillusion and sorrow, it was not likely that the sentiment should depart. Caeiro never returned to the splendid nonmysticism of *The Keeper of Sheep.*" Pessoa writing as Campos concurred with this judgment, but noted that these are "among the world's great love poems, for they are love poems by virtue of being about love and not by virtue of being poems. The poet loved because he loved, and not because love exists."

"Now that I feel love. . . ." Variant of "I were seeing something new" in l. 4: "life were completely new."

"Unable to sleep. . . ." In the penultimate line, after writing the Portuguese equivalent of "think about her," the author crossed out the preposition.

Uncollected Poems. "Miscellaneous poems that don't form a whole" is the more exact meaning of *Poemas Inconjuntos,* the Portuguese title for this third section of Caeiro's work. The following poems were published in the magazine *Athena* 5, in 1925: "The astonishing reality of things," "When spring arrives," "If, after I die . . . ," "You speak of civilization . . . ," "Truth, falsehood . . . ," "Hillside shepherd . . . ," "Between what I see . . . ," and "You say I'm something more." Pessoa scribbled in pencil some possible revisions to these poems in a copy of *Athena* 5. I have translated the poems as they were published.

"What's my life worth? . . ." Variant of "who after all is savvy" in the final line: "who is of the same opinion."

"I'm not in a hurry. . . ." Variants of the last line: "And we live as wanderers, far from our body [reality]."

"Live, you say, in the present." Variants of "the time that measures them" in l. 4: "the time we assign to them"; "the time where they are." Variant of "in my awareness of what exists" in l. 9: "in my scheme."

RICARDO REIS

The twenty-eight poems of Ricardo Reis published by Pessoa in magazines were designated as "odes," and they share many thematic and formal characteristics with those of Horace. Twenty of them were published in *Athena* 1, in 1924, as the heteronym's "First book of Odes," and other such books were supposed to follow. Nearly all of Reis's odes rigorously follow a metrical pattern—with lines of ten and six syllables predominating—but do not rhyme. Syntax is often crunched, or inverted—a characteristic less apparent in the translations, since English is less flexible when it comes to word order. Virtually all the poems published here are classifiable as Horatian odes, with the exception of "The Chess Players," whose twelve stanzas (suggestive, perhaps, of the triadic structure of Pindar's odes) are of unequal length.

The following odes were published in *Athena* 1, in 1924: "I love the roses . . . ," "Remember, with quick steps . . . ," "Lost from the way . . . ," "Securely I sit . . . ," "I want the flower . . . ," "The new summer . . . ," "How short a time . . . ," "Plowing his scant field . . . ," and "Don't try to build. . . ."

"Each thing, in its time. . . ." Variant of ll. 11–12: "Let's not push our voice / Higher than a secret." Variant of the last three lines of the sixth stanza: "We picked with a different consciousness / And a different way / Of looking at the world." Variant of the penultimate line of the sixth stanza: "And a different knowledge."

"Remember, with quick steps. . . ." The translation is of the revised version, which dates from the fall of 1923.

"We've always had. . . ." Variant of the word "confident" in l. 1: "troubled." Variant of the last two lines: "To wherever they want / And we don't want."

"Lost from the way. . . ." The translation is of the revised version, which dates from 1923–1924.

"A verse repeating. . . ." Variant of ll. 4–5: "And the soul's courtyard, / Vacant and sunlit. . . ."

"I don't want. . . ." Variant of ll. 1–3: "I don't want the presents / By which you pretend, sincerely, / To give what you give me."

"I want the flower. . . ." In the original Portuguese, an adjective describing the addressee of this ode is masculine in gender. Álvaro de Campos, in a prose piece "outing" Ricardo Reis, cites this grammatical detail to support his contention that Lydia, Chloe, and a third maiden invoked by the classicist poet were a ruse for his real romantic interest: young men.

"The new summer. . . ." The Latin epigraph appears on the manuscript but was not published with the ode in *Athena*, perhaps because Caeiro had not yet been publicly revealed. (Reis's public début was in the first issue of *Athena*, in 1924, Caeiro's in the fourth issue of the same magazine, in 1925.)

"Hour by hour. . . ." Variant of the last two lines: "Let us wrap, in the cup of our cold hands, / The flame of the uncertain hour."

"Already over my vain brow." Published in *Presença* 10, in 1928.

"Fruits are given. . . ." Variant of ll. 9–10: "Ah, against great opposition you cannot / Create more than doomed intentions!"

"To nothing. . . ." Published in *Presença* 6, in 1927.

"The fleeting track. . . ." Published in *Presença* 10, in 1928.

"When, Lydia. . . ." Published in *Presença* 31–32, in 1931.

"Hesitant, as if. . . ." Published in *Presença* 31–32, in 1931.

"Nothing of nothing. . . ." Variant of l. 6: "Decreed laws, tall statues, finished odes—."

"To be great. . . ." Published in *Presença* 37, in 1933.

"All I ask the gods. . . ." Crossed out on the manuscript, which typically means that the author made a typed copy, perhaps with revisions, but in this case no typed copy is known to have survived.

ÁLVARO DE CAMPOS

Álvaro de Campos was the most prolific of the poetic heteronyms. Pessoa's longest poem, "The Maritime Ode," was signed by the naval engineer, whose initial task—according to plans drawn up by his inventor—was to produce five "futurist odes." The only odes completed were "The Triumphal Ode" and "The Maritime Ode." "Time's Passage" and "Salutation to Walt Whitman," both left as numerous, unconnected pieces, may be considered odes in Campos's futurist manner, and there are other, fragmentary odes whose various pieces date mostly from 1914–16. In 1923 Campos, after a fallow period as a poet, returned to active duty with a less flamboyant style. His poems tended to become shorter as time went on, and the late poem that begins "How long it's been . . ." (p. 254) complains about the fact.

"Opiary." This poem, fictionally dated 1914, was actually written in 1915, for publication in the inaugural issue of the magazine *Orpheu*, where it was dedicated to Mário de Sá-Carneiro. In his 13 January 1935 letter to Adolfo Casais Monteiro, Pessoa explained: "When it came time to publish *Orpheu*, we had to find something at the last minute to fill out the issue, and so I suggested to Sá-Carneiro that I write an 'old' poem of Álvaro de Campos—a poem such as Álvaro de Campos would have written before meeting Caeiro and falling under his influence. That's how I came to write 'Opiary,' in which I tried to incorporate all the latent tendencies of Álvaro de Campos that would eventually be revealed but that still showed no hint of contact with his master Caeiro. Of all the poems I've written, this was the one that gave me the most trouble, because of the twofold depersonalization it required. But I don't think it turned out badly, and it does show us Álvaro in the bud."

Pessoa translated about five stanzas of the poem into English. He preceded his translation with the following note: "The word 'Opiary,' of course, does not exist in English. But neither does 'Opiário' (of which 'opiary' is the exact translation) exist in Portuguese. The translator has followed the neologism of the original."

"Triumphal Ode." Published in *Orpheu* 1, in 1915. According to Campos's "biography," he wrote the poem in London in June of 1914, upon his return from the Orient. It was indeed written in that month, but in Lisbon. It was the first Campos poem produced by Pessoa.

"Excerpts from Two Odes." In the manuscript the title, which is Pessoa's, is followed by a parenthetical indication: "conclusions to two odes, naturally." Pessoa apparently gave up on the idea of writing the rest of the two odes, whose "conclusions" read as polished, complete poems. In a letter to a friend, he referred to the first excerpt as an "Ode to Night." (My translation is based on a version of the two "excerpts" published in 1938. Some editions of Campos's poetry opt for a slightly different version, found among Pessoa's papers.) Cesário Verde (1855–1886), mentioned in the first stanza of the second "excerpt," was the most modern Portuguese poet of his generation. "The Feeling of a Westerner," his greatest poem, evokes the urban reality of nineteenth-century Lisbon with vivid, concrete imagery. Verde, an important influence on the poetry of cosmopolitan Campos, is also named in a poem of Caeiro and in passages from *The Book of Disquiet*.

"Maritime Ode." Published in *Orpheu* 2, in 1915, with a dedication to Santa Rita Pintor (1889–1918), a painter and member of the *Orpheu* group. The town of Almada, mentioned in the last third of the poem, lies on the far side of the Tagus River in relation to Lisbon.

"Salutation to Walt Whitman." As explained in the Notes on the Selection, Editing, and Translation (pp. xli–xliv), Pessoa wrote more than twenty passages for this unfinished poem. The majority of the passages are not even complete units in themselves, being sprinkled with blank spaces for missing words and unfinished sentences. Many are handwritten, and certain phrases and even entire stanzas have not thus far been convincingly deciphered. The "Salutation" presented here excludes the sketchier material and those portions of the text for which reliable transcriptions have not been established. Diamonds have been placed between the separate passages, whose order is my own responsibility. Omitted phrases or sections (where the manuscripts are partly or wholly illegible) are indicated by three dots (. . .);

lacunae in the original text are indicated by five dots (. . . . .). Other editorial interventions are indicated in the notes that follow.

"Portugal, Infinity. . . ." Rua do Ouro, mentioned in the fourth stanza of this passage, is one of the main streets in downtown Lisbon.

"And so it's to you. . . ." In the manuscript there is a blank space after the word translated as "carriage" in the fourth line; the author no doubt intended to complete it with an adjective.

"Gateway to everything!" An unfinished line following the seventh line of the third stanza has been suppressed.

"Time for our vitality. . . ." Variant of the last line: "When does it leave?"

"Hup-hup? . . . " The phrase "caresser of life," in l. 12, is from Whitman's *Song of Myself*, section 13. The closing parenthetical mark at the end of the ninth line in the last stanza is there by conjecture; the author opened but neglected to close the parenthesis.

"All along the wharf. . . ." Undated but presumed to be a relatively early poem.

"Lisbon Revisited (1923)." Published in the magazine *Contemporânea*, in 1923.

"Lisbon Revisited (1926)." Published in *Contemporânea*, in 1926.

"If you want to kill yourself. . . ." Written ten years to the day after the suicide of Pessoa's closest friend, the writer Mário de Sá-Carneiro.

"Squib." Published in *Presença* 18, in 1929. A manuscript copy of the poem bears the title "Futurist Squib." David Lloyd George (1863–1945), from Wales, was head of Britain's Liberal Party and served as prime minister from 1916 to 1922. Aristide Briand (1862–1932), French premier in World War I, won the Nobel Peace Prize in 1926.

"Clouds." Variant of "symmetrical" in l. 9: "synthetic."

"Note." Published in *Presença* 20, in 1929.

"Yes it's me. . . ." Variant of "adult tears" in the ninth line from the end: "dead tears."

"Ah, a Sonnet . . ." Published in *Presença* 34, in 1932.

"My heart. . . ." Undated, but apparently a companion to the previous sonnet.

"Speak softly. . . ." Variant of "foam" in l. 9: "flesh."

"The stillness of midnight. . . ." Variant of "speak to me" in l. 17: "arouse me."

"Homecoming." In the manuscript the title is followed by the parenthetical phrase, in English, "end of the book."

"Là-bas, Je Ne Sais Où . . ." The title means "Over there, I don't know where."

FERNANDO PESSOA–HIMSELF

A Portuguese term akin to "Pessoa–himself" was used by the poet to distinguish the literary persona called Fernando Pessoa from the heteronyms. This persona had, in turn, various "subpersonalities," such as Pessoa the lyrical poet (whose "lyricism" was largely concerned with existential issues), Pessoa the esoteric poet, Pessoa the experimentalist, Pessoa the nationalist, or mystical nationalist, Pessoa the popular poet, and Pessoa the humorist. These last two facets, not represented in the present volume, gave rise to several hundred traditional folk quatrains, as well as some light and humorous verse, sometimes written for family members.

Songbook. In a letter from 1932 to João Gaspar Simões, his future biographer, Pessoa expressed his intention of publishing, in a large volume titled *Songbook*, "a number of my many miscellaneous poems, which are too diverse to be classified except in that inexpressive way." We don't know how diversified such a volume might have been. It may have included his esoteric and metaphysical poems, which are usually rhymed and metered, like his more obviously lyric poetry, and it might even have included free-verse poems written for the most part in the 1910s ("Slanting Rain," "Diary in the Shade") or toward the end of his life ("Freedom," "*Un Soir à Lima*"). For all its "inexpressive" generality, the title *Songbook* evokes a specific leitmotif of the would-be collection's poems, in which there are frequent mentions of music, musical instruments, and musicians.

"O church bell. . . ." This and "Swamps of yearnings . . . ," the first poems published by Pessoa as an adult, in 1914, appeared as a diptych under the general title "Twilight Impressions." "O church bell of my village" was republished in 1925, with several changes in the third stanza, reflected in my translation. Pessoa wrote João Gaspar Simões that the "village" of the poem was Chiado, the centrally located neighborhood of Lisbon where Pessoa was born and spent his first years; the "church bell" was of the Chiado church where he was baptized.

"Abdication." Published in 1920.

"Swamps of yearnings. . . ." This poem first circulated among Pessoa's friends under the title "Swamps," which gave rise to the term Swampism, an exacerbated post-symbolist aesthetic typified in the poem and cultivated for several years by Pessoa and some of his literary compeers, especially Mário de Sá-Carneiro. Published in 1914 with "O church bell . . ." (see the penultimate note).

"Slanting Rain." Published in *Orpheu* 2, in 1915. Álvaro de Campos explains, in his "Notes for the Memory of My Master Caeiro," that Fernando Pessoa, after meeting Alberto Caeiro and hearing him recite *The Keeper of Sheep*, "went home in a fever (the one he was born with) and wrote the six poems of 'Slanting Rain' in one go. . . . They were a direct result of the spiritual shock he experienced mere moments after that meeting occurred." The poems were published with the subtitle "Intersectionist Poems," intersectionism being the name of yet another short-lived artistic "movement" conceived and promoted by Pessoa, who imagined the principle being applied to various types of art, and even beyond the arts. In his own intersectionist poetry, of which "Slanting Rain" is the best example, diverse spatial, temporal, and psychological planes intersect, without fusing. It can be thought of as a literary equivalent to Cubism.

"The Reaper." Published in 1916 and, with revisions, in 1925 (*Athena* 3, dated December 1924). The translation is of the final version.

"Passerby." The poem assumed its final shape, on which the translation is based, on 21 August 1921. It was classified by Pessoa, in a publication project, as one of his "Songs of Lisbon."

"The Scaffold." Published in *Presença* 31–32, in 1931.

"Her very being surprises." The woman referred to in this unusually erotic poem is undoubtedly Hanni Jaeger, the young and attractive German-American girlfriend of the English magus Aleister Crowley. (See the Chronology for the years 1929–30.) The couple arrived in Lisbon eight days before this poem was written.

"There's no one who loves me." Variant of the final line: "Feeling is another emotion."

"I come to the window." Variant of the final line: "And no one gives me anything."

"Autopsychography." Published in *Presença* 32, in 1932.

"I'm guided only by reason." Published in 1932.

"Initiation." Published in *Presença* 35, in 1932.

"What I write's not mine. . . ." The manuscript contains, in parentheses, two possible closing couplets, one of which I've used for the English translation. Using the other couplet, the last three lines could be translated as:

> From the dust I am
> And made me into a cloud in a moment
> Of thinking.

Pessoa might, in the end, have rejected the parenthetical additions, ending the poem with the fourteenth line ("From the dust I am").

"Senhor Silva." Classified by Pessoa, in a publication project, as one of his "Songs of Lisbon."

"In this world. . . ." Variant of "grins and appearances" in l. 5: "grins of gnomes."

"Advice." Published in November of 1935 in *Sudoeste* 3, a magazine edited by Almada Negreiros, a writer and painter who was part of the *Orpheu* group.

"At the Tomb of Christian Rosenkreutz." This trio of sonnets was given to Almada Negreiros to be published in *Sudoeste* 3 (see previous note) but did not actually see print until 1942. The *Fama Fraternitatis*, published in German in 1614 and in Latin a year later, was the first public document about the Rosicrucians. It tells the story of Christian Rosenkreutz (identified only by his initials), who was purportedly born into a poor but noble German family (in 1378, according to other documents), traveled as a young man to Damascus, where he studied with astrologers and physicians, then to Egypt and finally Morocco, where he spent two years in Fez learning the alchemical arts. Returning to Germany by way of Spain, he founded the Rosy Cross brotherhood. The passage of the *Fama* in the epigraph describes the discovery of Christian Rosenkreutz's tomb 120 years after his death.

Pessoa read a number of books about Rosicrucianism and was keenly interested in the symbolic import of the Rose and the Cross. The following passage, from among his writings on Rosicrucian philosophy, is helpful for understanding the three sonnets:

> The twin essence, masculine and feminine, of God—the Cross. The created world, the Rose, crucified in God.
>
> Creation is not an emanation but, more properly, a *limitation*, a negation of God by himself. It would be more accurate to say that the universe is the negation of God, or the death of God. But since the negation or death of God is necessarily divine, the universe contains a divine element which is the Law—an abstract and, as it were, *absent* element.
>
> God's only miracle is the universe.
>
> The Law, *Fatum*, is an abstract element of God, whereby God is incorporeally manifested to the world. In opposition to this Law stands Christ, i.e., the desire for a Return to God, the desire for Freedom, for not having any *Fatum*.

"Freedom." This was the first of many anti-Salazar poems written by Pessoa in his last year. The penultimate line is a direct dig at the dictator, who began his meteoric rise to power as Portugal's finance minister, in 1928. This and other such poems were largely motivated by Salazar's warning, in a speech delivered on 21 February 1935, that the works of writers should be sensitive to and even promote the "moral and patriotic principles" of his so-called New State (Estado Novo). The Prime Minister ended his speech with the quotation from Seneca that appears here as the poem's epigraph. Pessoa, who merely indicated on his manuscript that an unspecified citation from Seneca was to precede the poem, surely had this "re-citation" in mind.

About King Sebastian, see the note on p. 432 to the poem in *Message* titled "Sebastian, King of Portugal."

"Un Soir à Lima." The title is from a piece of music by Félix Godefroid that Pessoa's mother played on the piano in Durban, South Africa. Pessoa wrote ten or so passages for this poem—some left in the rough and with lacunae, others that were reworked into a more or less finished state—but never attempted to organize them into a finished whole. Luís Prista, who first deciphered and published the various passages, arranged them in a convincing narrative. I have followed his arrangement but excluded some of the redundant and less finished sections, and I've separated the discrete passages by diamonds. The date appears on the last passage.

The "little ones" of the third passage are Pessoa's half brothers, Luís Miguel and João Maria, who would both have been less than five years old. "This girl" is Pessoa's half sister, Henriqueta Madalena, who would have been seven or eight.

"There are sicknesses. . . ." The last poem Pessoa wrote in Portuguese.

Message. The only book of Portuguese verse published by Pessoa consists of forty-four poems written between 1913 and 1934, some of which were published in magazines. The book's working title, "Portugal," was changed to *Message* in the fall of 1934, when the book was already in production. Awarded a prize by the Secretariat of National Propaganda for poetry that was "deeply Portuguese" and inspired by a "high sense of nationalist exaltation," *Message* retold Portuguese history from a mystical point of view, investing historical facts and national legends with symbolic significance. Pessoa, while admitting in a letter dated 13 January 1935 that it was not, in personal terms, a felicitous publishing début, believed that "it coincided with a critical moment . . . in the transformation of the national subconscious." That belief was badly shaken if not altogether crushed in the succeeding months, when he realized the true extent of Salazar's program of control and censure (see the Chronology for 1935).

"Coat of Arms: The Castles." Seven castles form the outer field of the Portuguese coat of arms.

"Coat of Arms: The Shields." Five shields occupy the inner field of the Portuguese coat of arms.

"Ulysses." According to legend, for which there's no historical basis, the Greek hero, in his wanderings after the Trojan War, reached the Portuguese coast and founded Olisipo, which later came to be known as Lisbon.

"Viriathus." A shepherd and chief of the Lusitanians, inhabitants of what later came to be Portugal, Viriathus managed to resist the Roman legions for many years. After a series of humiliating defeats, the Romans reportedly bribed several of Viriathus' comrades to assassinate him in his sleep, in 139 B.C.

"Count Henry." This French count (1066–1112) married Teresa, the natural daughter of Alfonso VI, king of Castile and León, and in December of 1095 he was made governor of Portucale, the territory between the Minho and Douro rivers, and Coimbra, below the Douro. Despite its feudal obligations to the Spanish crown, the territory became semi-autonomous, initiating the break of Portugal from Spain.

"Sebastian, King of Portugal." This young king (1554–1578), fanatically nationalistic and religious, a mystic and a dreamer, led thousands of soldiers to their near total capture or slaughter in an ill-conceived expedition to reconquer lost Portuguese territories in Morocco. Two years later, in 1580, debilitated Portugal fell under Spanish rule, regaining its independence only sixty years later. A myth arose that Sebastian had escaped death and taken refuge on a desert isle, from where he would return one foggy morning as the *Encoberto*, the Hidden One, to free Portugal from Spanish domination. As the centuries passed, the myth of the king's return acquired new, symbolic interpretations.

"Horizon." First published in the magazine *Contemporânea*, in 1922.

"The West." Published, with slight differences, in *Contemporânea*, in 1922.

"The Fifth Empire." The "one who dreamed" of the penultimate stanza was Nebuchadnezzar, king of Babylon. His dream, as interpreted by the biblical prophet Daniel and understood by Pessoa, supplied the mythic underpinnings of the Fifth Empire doctrine, according to which Portugal, through its literature and culture, would dominate the rest of Europe. See the Introduction for a fuller explanation.

Ruba'iyat. Inspired by FitzGerald's rendering into English of the

ruba'iyat of Omar Khayyam, Pessoa wrote close to two hundred po-
ems in the same style, each a single quatrain with an *aaba* rhyme
scheme. The thematic content of these ruba'iyat—life's vanity and
brevity, and the wisdom of enjoying the little we have—recalls the sen-
timents expressed in the poetry of Ricardo Reis, and it's worth noting
that the longest poem by the classicist heteronym, "The Chess Play-
ers," is set in Persia.

The ruba'iyat are in chronological order. The first three, published
by Pessoa in *Contemporânea*, in 1926, are probably the first three he
wrote. The other ones published here were written between November
of 1928 and October of 1935. The epigraph to the Introduction, also
a ruba'i, is undated.

"Don't say that the soul. . . ." Variant of "You know only" in the
last line: "All you have is."

Faust. Pessoa wrote around two hundred passages—ranging from a
single phrase to several pages in length—for this verse drama inspired by
Goethe's *Faust*. In fact Pessoa planned to write three different Faustian
dramas, and he drafted a synopsis of the first one, which was to repre-
sent "the struggle between Life and the Intelligence," with the latter,
embodied by Faust, always losing to the former. The general theme of
the first *Faust* is the mystery of the world, the mystery of existence,
"since this is the central theme of the Intelligence." Unable to under-
stand Life, the Intelligence (in the person of Faust) sets out to control
Life. Failing abysmally, it then tries to adapt to Life, epitomized as the
experience of Love. Again it fails. In the end Death arrives, and Faust
faces, with redoubled horror, not only the mystery of the known world
but also the mystery of the unknown.

Attempts have been made to order the *Faust* material according to
the plot just described, but the fragmentary passages left by Pessoa—
written at random and over the course of his entire adult life, beginning
at age twenty—don't amount to anything like a play. The passages
translated here, all narrated by Faust and nearly all of them in blank
verse, have been ordered without regard to where Pessoa might have
placed them in one or another of his three projected *Faust*s.

"The only mystery in the universe." Variant of "the soul's body" in
the last line of the second stanza: "earth of the soul."

"Life's brief and fleeting nature proves." Dated 3 March 1928.

"Ah, everything is symbol and analogy!" Dated 9 November 1932.
Variant of "the mother illusion of this illusion" in the final line: "the
reality of this illusion."

"In me." Dated 6 November 1912.

"Oh, to drink life in one gulp . . ." Variant of l. 17: "While I keep a strong personality." Variant of "to hell itself" in the final line: "to a literal hell."

ENGLISH POEMS

Almost all the poetry Pessoa wrote up until his twentieth year was in English, and he continued to write assiduously in that language until 1921. At that point his poetic production in English waned, but it never ceased. His last English poem, a simple love lyric, was written on November 22, 1935, a week before he died.

Alexander Search. See the Introduction for information on this English-language heteronym.

35 Sonnets. Self-published as a chapbook in 1918 (see the Introduction). Pessoa left a copy of the book with some neatly written revisions that were clearly intended for the typesetter of a new edition (never realized). The four sonnets published here include those revisions.

The Mad Fiddler. Pessoa carefully organized this collection of fifty-three poems, written between 1911 and 1917, and tried to place it with an English publisher, in vain (see the Introduction).

BIBLIOGRAPHY

PUBLISHED SOURCES FOR THE POEMS

Pessoa, Fernando. *Canções de Beber*, ed. Maria Aliete Galhoz. Lisbon: Assírio & Alvim, 2003. Contains Pessoa's ruba'iyat in the manner of Omar Khayyam.

———. *Fausto: Tragédia Subjectiva*, ed. Teresa Sobral Cunha. Lisbon: Presença, 1988.

———. *Mensagem*, ed. Fernando Cabral Martins. Lisbon: Assírio & Alvim, 1997.

———. *Obra Essencial de Fernando Pessoa*, vols. II, IV, and VI, ed. Richard Zenith. Lisbon: Assírio & Alvim, 2006–2007.

———. *Obra Poética*, ed. Maria Aliete Galhoz. 7th ed. Rio de Janeiro: Nova Aguilar, 1977.

———. *Poemas de Fernando Pessoa 1921–1930*, ed. Ivo Castro. Lisbon: INCM, 2001.

———. *Poemas de Fernando Pessoa 1931–1933*, ed. Ivo Castro. Lisbon: INCM, 2004.

———. *Poemas de Fernando Pessoa 1934–1935*, ed. Luís Prista. Lisbon: INCM, 2000.

———. *Poesia, Alberto Caeiro*, eds. Fernando Cabral Martins and Richard Zenith. 2nd ed. Lisbon: Assírio & Alvim, 2004.

———. *Poesia, Alexander Search*, ed. Luísa Freire. Lisbon: Assírio & Alvim, 1999.

———. *Poesia, Álvaro de Campos*, ed. Teresa Rita Lopes. Lisbon: Assírio & Alvim, 2002.

———. *Poesia Inglesa (I)*, ed. Luísa Freire. Lisbon: Assírio & Alvim, 2000.

———. *Poesia, Ricardo Reis*, ed. Manuela Parreira da Silva. Lisbon: Assírio & Alvim, 2000.

OTHER EDITIONS CONSULTED

Pessoa, Fernando. *Poemas Ingleses*, vols. I–II, ed. João Dionísio. Lisbon: INCM, 1993, 1997.

———. *Poemas Ingleses*, vol. III, eds. Fernando Gomes and Marcus Angioni. Lisbon: INCM, 1999.

———. *Poemas de Ricardo Reis*, ed. Luiz Fagundes Duarte. Lisbon: INCM, 1994.